CATHERINE BREESE DAVIS

ON THE LIFE AND WORK OF AN AMERICAN MASTER

ISBN: 978-0-9641454-6-7

Published by Pleiades Press
Department of English
The University of Central Missouri
Warrensburg, Missouri 64093

Distributed by Small Press Distribution (SPD) and to subscribers
of *Pleiades: Literature in Context.*

Cover and interior book design by Martin Rock.
Cover photograph by Marie Pelletier.

2 4 6 8 9 7 5 3 1
First Peleiades Press Printing, 2015

The Unsung Masters Series brings the work of great, out-of-print,
little-known writers to new readers. Each volume in the Series
includes a large selection of the author's original writing, as well as
essays on the writer, interviews with people who knew the writer,
photographs, and ephemera. The curators of the Unsung Masters
Series are always interested in suggestions for future volumes.

Invaluable financial support for this project has been provided by the
National Endowment for the Arts and the Missouri Arts Council, a
state agency. Our immense gratitude to both organizations.

CATHERINE BREESE DAVIS
ON THE LIFE AND WORK OF AN AMERICAN MASTER

Edited by Martha Collins, Kevin Prufer, & Martin Rock

THE UNSUNG MASTERS SERIES

PLEIADES
P R E S S

CONTENTS

INTRODUCTION

The book you are holding began like every book in the Unsung Masters Series: with a recommendation between friends and a casual conversation. This one occurred over dinner in Cambridge on a rainy winter night in 2013. If my recollection is right, we were well into a bottle of red wine at a small restaurant just off Harvard Square when Martha Collins mentioned Catherine Davis, a writer I'd never heard of.

Martha's and Catherine's lives had intersected in the 1960s in Iowa City, and then later, in Boston. In both places, Davis had made an indelible impression: she was a brilliant, sophisticated poet with a fully mature voice and a fierce disposition. Catherine was considerably older than the other Iowa City students, Martha said, and had impressed her as highly accomplished, in part because she'd arrived after studying with Yvor Winters under what would become the Stegner Fellowship. She was enviably well published, having already had poems in *The New Yorker*, *The Paris Review*, and Hall, Pack, & Simpson's seminal anthology, *New Poets of England and America*. And, Martha said, she had a deep understanding of the vagaries of traditional form, of meter and music.

We didn't have her poems at the table that evening, so the conversation hovered around Martha's descriptions of Catherine's early, highly controlled classical formalism, her mastery of rhetoric and diction, and most of all the complexity of thought and emotion that lived in her work, even as that work progressed toward a looser formalism and an often intensely personal free verse. Though she had been recognized by a number of eminent mentors and other writers, her life in Iowa City began to grow turbulent. She struggled with alcoholism and emotional problems and eventually lost touch with many of her friends—though never with Donald Justice, who remained a consistent supporter of her work until the end of her life. It was a memorable story—sad and, at the same time, inspiring.

Explicit in our conversation was the idea of considering Catherine Davis for the Unsung Masters Series, provided that I first concurred with Martha about the quality of the work. Martha had heard from a friend that a manuscript of Davis's work had been collected and edited, but for reasons that weren't entirely clear, had not found a publisher. She thought there might have been some difficulty with acquiring rights.

———◆———

The Unsung Masters Series exists to bring the work of great writers to the attention of readers who will certainly otherwise never discover them. Our rules are simple, if deliberately a little vague:

First, the writer in question may not have a book in print. Or, if the writer has a book in print, it must be exceedingly hard to find. (In one instance, a poet's book was technically in print because four copies sat on a shelf in his publisher's office in Cleveland, where'd they'd remained since 1977.)

Second, the writer must be almost completely unknown. "What do we mean by 'unknown'?" I once asked Wayne Miller, the series co-curator. "How about this," he said: "In any random gathering of ten voracious literary readers, none of them should have ever heard of our author's name." "Sounds good," I said.

Third (and this is where things get tricky): we've got to be able to discover a few serious readers who know the work well enough to write thoughtfully about it. Ideally we'll also be able to find someone who knew the writer well outside her writing life, and who can give us a sense of the writer's identity beyond the page. And if we can find ephemera—photographs, drafts of manuscripts, journal entries—that helps, too.

The idea for the Series, finally, is not just to publish the work of an interesting, out-of-print author. We're more ambitious than that. We want to do our best to offer readers a sense of the writer as a person—her concerns, passions, and questions, the life behind the work that informs and deepens the reading experience. One critic has described the series as "archaeological," and I don't disagree. So much of these projects feels like excavation, unearthing and piecing together what a living human being has left behind—and, in so doing, creating a picture of something larger, a worldview and a sensibility that might otherwise disappear.

———————•———————

We weren't the first to try to put together a volume of Catherine Breese Davis's poetry. A quick Internet search turned up a 2008 article in *Stanford News* about another attempt to bring a large body of Davis's work into print. Two other editors—Helen Pinkerton Trimpi (who was at Stanford with Davis) and Suzanne Doyle—had already drawn together a collection of Davis's poetry. Rights acquisition, however, had become a major hurdle for them and, ultimately, had kept the poems from finding a publisher. "The publishers they [...] approached," the article asserted, "are jittery that an heir may suddenly appear and sue for copyright violation."

Trimpi and Doyle were easy to contact and responded to our project with enthusiasm and helpfulness, forwarding to us information about their search for rights as well as a copy of their manuscript, which strongly favored the most formally rigorous of Davis's poetry. They'd made some progress in finding the name and probably defunct address of an heir—Davis's nephew, Roger Mitchell—but were unable to make contact or acquire rights. Even after enlisting a genealogist and lawyer, the project languished.

I began where they left off, with extensive searches of public property records in Texas, where Suzanne thought Mitchell might be living. This meant calling one Roger Mitchell after another—every Roger Mitchell who lived within about 100 miles of any place our specific Roger

Mitchell may or may not have owned a piece of property, in Texas, then Georgia, then Oklahoma.

Several Roger Mitchells seemed unsure about whether they may have had a relative named Catherine who wrote poetry, though a couple promised to investigate. One did have a dead aunt Kate. "I don't think she wrote poetry, though," he said. When we finally found the right Roger Mitchell, in North Texas (discovered through a mundane internet bulletin board posting still cached on the web from many years ago), he was easy to work with and seemed happy to see his aunt's poetry brought to readers.

From here, Martha and I began gathering friends, critics, and acquaintances: Suzanne Doyle and Helen Pinkerton Trimpi; poet Kenneth Fields, who knew her work through Yvor Winters; poets Kathe Davis and Michael van Walleghen, friends from Iowa; poet Carol Moldaw and critic William Edinger; and most of all, Marie Pelletier, Davis's companion for many years, who eventually became absolutely central to the project, offering boxes of notebooks, journals, drafts, and photographs, and who consented to be interviewed by Martin Rock (a University of Houston PhD student who joined the project just as it was getting off the ground) and myself.

Along the way, we also had to contend with selecting from among competing versions of Davis's poems, often revised repeatedly over many years. Even deciding what to call her— "Catherine Davis," "Catherine B. Davis," "Catherine Breese Davis"—raised questions. The poet herself was inconsistent in her published work and her unpublished manuscripts.

Marie Pelletier's contribution to this book can't be overstated. She has been the source of a wealth of personal information that no other living person could have provided, for none of Davis's friends were as close to her over the years as was Marie. She has stood by to offer corrections where we've gone astray and insights where we needed them. And the long interview that begins the prose section of this book offers fascinating insights into the character and life of our subject.

As a happy afterthought, we have learned as this book goes to press that Catherine Davis's papers—her journals, drafts of poems, letters, etc.—will soon be archived at Stanford University's library, where they will be made available to those who wish to look further into Catherine Davis's life and work.

—KP

A NOTE ON THE TEXT

The compilation of poems that follows is necessarily selective. The sources we have used include:

1. Three letterpress pamphlets Davis herself printed: *The Leaves* (1960), *Second Beginnings* (1961), and *Under This Lintel* (1962). The first two were published in Washington, D.C., the third in Iowa City. The pamphlets were never distributed, and are virtually impossible to find.

2. A manuscript of poems compiled for publication by Suzanne Doyle and Helen Pinkerton in 2006, which includes all of the poems in the pamphlets and other early poems, and some selections from *Yes Is a Very Big Word*, the selected poems

compiled by Davis (#4 below).

3. *From the Narrow House to the Wide World*, a collection compiled by Davis in the late 1960s and submitted for publication in 1970.

4. *Yes Is A Very Big Word*, a selected poems Davis finished compiling in 1995.

5. Handwritten notebooks in which Davis wrote drafts of her poems, currently in the possession of Marie Pelletier.

6. A few magazine or anthology versions of poems (especially "She").

Our examination and comparison of texts have not been exhaustive. We have not consulted Davis's MA thesis, *The First Step*, located at the University of Iowa libraries, nor have we consulted most of the magazines and anthologies in which poems originally appeared. Although one of us has read all of Davis's notebooks, journals, and papers, we chose material from them primarily on the basis of what seemed interesting to us.

Our choice of poems has been similarly personal, as has our choice of versions: in the many cases in which the sources used different versions of a particular poem, we simply chose the one we liked best. When later versions exhibited extensive revision, this was often but not always the first version. On the other hand, we have often opted for later versions in smaller matters such as punctuation, and have very occasionally assembled a "hybrid" version in regard to such matters.

The order of the collection is also something of a hybrid. On the one hand, we wanted to give some sense of the development of Davis's work, as well as the life it reflects, and thus aimed for a rough chronology; on the other, we wished to extend the same attention to the ordering of poems that Davis herself did in assembling her several collections (not all of which are available even in her papers, where several tables of contents appear without poems), and thus to create a unified work.

Roughly speaking, the poems up through "Late" (p. 40) all come from the three pamphlets or other pre-1962 publications, though they are not in the order in which they initially or later appeared. The poems through "A Small River in Iowa and the Wide World" (p. 58) were at least conceived before Davis left Iowa City, as were several poems that appear later in the manuscript. Most of the remaining part of the manuscript, up through "The Willows in Winter in the Boston Public Garden" (p. 88), attempts to balance the formal and free verse poems that Davis was writing simultaneously until the late 1970s, when she stopped writing altogether until, in the 1990s, she wrote the penultimate poem in this collection.

—MC

THE POEMS OF CATHERINE BREESE DAVIS

To the memory of J. V. Cunningham
poet, scholar, teacher, and friend

and to Beth Nelson
who for several years was
the first, best, and sometimes only
reader of my poems

and to Don Justice
for decades of generosity,
forbearance, and timely encouragement

—Catherine Davis, dedication for
Yes Is a Very Big Word (1995 manuscript)

BEFORE YOU ENTER

You know how it is to hold in mind
A place—a house or a river scene—
That keeps an earlier time intact
For years, and then to go back and find
Either you had made it out to be
Something it never was, or in fact
It's gone. Or irrelevant. Or new
High-rises dwarf it, alter the view.

So it is now with me. What seemed fixed,
My version of it, has come apart.

Consider, before you enter here,
Whatever motives you have, how mixed
And yet divided these feelings are.
It's nothing new, this being unclear—
Estranged, yet haunted.
                              Nothing to do
But let it go at last. Or try to.

INDOLENCE

I drowse, but hear the sibilance
Of oaks. Indolent August days
             Suggest my ways,
And everything I do, I do by chance.

Today I wandered in a grove
Where all sound was indefinite,
             For nothing fit
But revery and oracles of Jove.

I do not think Dodona spoke
Less vaguely than the nameless wood
             In which I stood
And heard the wind disturb the drowsy oak.

In idle half-intentions now,
Not in the underspeech of leaves,
             The future grieves,
Lifts and subsides—a casual, shaken bough.

THE LEAVES

That time the leaves suffused
The summer light with shade;
Being by shade bemused,
    We all in shadow lay
    That deepened day by day.

It seemed that darkness, made
Of light, no light refused;
That burning motion, stayed
    In those still leaves, possessed
    The secret of all rest.

But when the leaves are blown,
They go not willfully;
Nor will they, left alone,
    Ponder the light, the shade.
    When cold and waste pervade

And alter them, they see
No semblance of their own
Full destitution; we,
    Necessitous, will find
    Some likeness for the mind.

As leaves no rest assure,
As light, unfleshed and stark,
Will bodiless endure
    The winter, but must go
    A ghost across the snow,

So we were but the mark
Of change, not more secure,
And not to love less dark,
    Who cast so full a shade,
    Being of such light made.

INSIGHTS

1.

Love is not blind, but overmuch
Given to darkness goes by touch.

2. *To a Little Editor*

You chose of all the poems I had sent
A few you thought were trinkets, but you meant
(You said) no slight. Merely, they were my best,
So strong that you would save them from the rest,
Ambitious of another vein, not fit
For my true quintessential trivial wit.
If this were malice (as it seemed to me),
Strange that the politics of poetry
That knows when to withhold, when to let fly,
Should reach one of so small account as I.
It could not be. Thus do we misconstrue.
Merely, though politic, you're fatuous too.

3. *Passerculi*

If you would have dark themes and high-flown words,
Great albatrosses drenched in sacredness,
Go read some other book; for I confess
I cannot make my verses to your taste.
And though they are not trifles made in haste,
Mine are to those such light things, little birds,
Sparrows among their kind, whose one last shift
Is shelter from the universal drift.

4. *KINDNESS*

Your kindness is no kindness now:
It is unkindness to allow
My unkind heart so to reveal
The differences it would conceal.
If I were, as I used to be,
As kind to you as you to me,
Or if I could but teach you how
To be unkind, as I am now,
That would be kindness of a kind,
To be again of a like mind.

5.

My self will flee, my shadow still pursue,
Whose self is but the shadow my self threw;
And while my unrest shall its rest undo,
My self, forsaking, still avenges you.

6.

They are not bees, this busy crowd;
They sting as hard and buzz as loud
And fly about but do not mean:
Neither the striving philistine,
On the level or on the take,
Nor all these scribblers on the make
Will ever bring, though some may thrive,
One drop of nectar to the hive.

7. *IMITATION OF SOME LINES BY CATULLUS*

Idleness, wretch, idleness ruins you!
Idleness works by more than mere inaction:
Exalts, among the great, great idlers, too,
And plunges you in riot and distraction.

8.

Beware, old scrounger, or, with winter come,
Your little impecuniosity
Will find at last the necessary sum
To cover all the waste there still must be:
All is the naked ground. And nothing, then,
Need fail you, who need never fail again.

9.

Comforting hope, how you have kept me warm!
Not that I have not gone in freezing storm,
Head down against the wind, flat broke and sore,
But that I did not see myself before
As this mere fool, huddled, a shivering form
In last year's ragged things, and nothing more.

10. *TO THE SPIRIT OF BAUDELAIRE*

Wind of the wing of madness! What is this?
O you that shuddered then, what manic bird?
What travesty, dark spirit, of the Word?

What last cold exhalation of your bliss?
What passage to what end? Speechless abyss.

11. IN NEW YORK

What can I do here? I could learn to lie;
Mouth Freud and Zen; rub shoulders at the "Y"
With this year's happy few; greet every hack—
The rough hyena, the young trimmer pack,
The Village idiot—with an equal eye;
And always scratch the true backscratcher's back.
All this, in second Rome, I'd learn to do;
Hate secretly and climb; get money; quit,
An absolutely stoic hypocrite.
This, but not more. New York is something new:
The toadies like the toads they toady to.

12.

Pity, Catullus, these late revelers
Who celebrate their passing with a shout,
These idle, disabused malingerers
Who wait defeat, as in a barbarous rout
Amid a wreck of cities, nations lost:
They are as faggots in a holocaust.
Pity, among the rest, this sparrow verse.

13. *HESPERIDES*

And must I all die? Herrick, there are tears
Which now not even your *thirty thousand years*,
Nor all your Western isles, is proof against—
Tears not to be denied, nor countenanced.
For who shall be the guardians of such gold?
The red sun rides the sea: the Nymphs are old.
If we haul anchor, ply the dusky oars
Outward and outward from the burnished shores,
Although the apples hang as now, as fair,
What sound will break the glowing silence there?
But all I know is that I do not know.
Let me write well, not weep, and leave it so.

14. *GUERCINO'S ET IN ARCADIA EGO*

Even in Arcady, the mouse, the fly,
And Death agape confront the passerby.

ROUTINE

Oppressive hours and days and years
Of days and hours of this routine,
Until what time may lie between
To this great mass adheres.

Continuous fatigue! The days
Fall but distend; the nights, inert,
Are dullness and can never hurt:
The sense of weight delays

The sense of time. Now, still and dense,
Like office dust in morning air,
Leading to nothing, not despair,
Indifference is immense.

PATIENCE

When I was young, I mastered all;
I put down fear and slew remorse,
Thinking by this to bend my course
To my own will, escape my fall.

The seasons' burdens, one by one,
Encumbered me; then everywhere
Was change, but in impassive air;
A sense of going had begun.

Leaves drifted in the air's delay;
Then, quickened, though the days were slow,
The blackbirds turned; I watched them go
And wondered at so short a stay;

And wondered more what patient flight
Sustained them, for the smooth wings knew
No pulsing terror as they flew,
Nor the fleet promptings of delight.

Their resignation knew no mood
Of mortal sadness for the year;
They neither fled nor lingered here—
Made perfect for vicissitude.

But we must go our way and lend
Patience impatient strength to bear
The seasons of the brutal air,
Although they fail us in the end.

DISCRETION

What I discern shall be my own.
Let him who cannot be alone
Be comforted, for he shall heed
Only what answers to his need.

My thoughts, I find, discomfit me;
But they are still good company,
And I could now almost forego
All company to keep them so.

But caution says, *Be more discreet;*
Good judgment whispers, *Self-conceit;*
Then I, not affably, admit
Discretion will have none of it.

Not affable; but if he finds
No heady meeting of the minds,
He still requires much give-and-take.
I do it for discretion's sake.

WHAT DOES IT MEAN?

after Thomas Wyatt

What does it mean? I lie awake;
My mind needs rest, my bones all ache:
So needy and so loath to take?
      What does it mean?

When I should be most comforted,
Covers and pillow, limbs and head,
Are every which way in the bed.
      What does it mean?

I toss, I turn, I cough, I curse;
I must, it seems, all night rehearse,
Revile my days and make them worse.
      What does it mean?

I doze a little, dream, and start:
The random terrors of the heart
Wake me—they take my daemon's part:
      What does it mean?

My daemon says they cheat, they lie,
Run from themselves, themselves awry,
Who say it's love that makes them cry
      What does it mean?

How little they must need to know!
Nothing but love can rouse them so,
When a whole life is touch and go.
      What does it mean?

Thus it is I spend the night,
Conscious that in my daemon's sight
The waking heart must see things right:
      What does it mean?

What does it matter that the past
And my own daemon hold me fast?
I shall get sleep enough at last.
      What does it mean?

OBSESSION

Tenacious, parasitic ghost,
You eat my substance steadily;
I who fear inanition most
Meet it in you engrossing me.

You share my narrow bed; you make
My thoughts your own, your own my blood;
Dire breath of evil, what can slake
Your dark thirst to consume my good?

That you are nothing, yet exist!
You feed as shadow on the light
And grow—on what shall I subsist?
You, the abhorred, besiege my sight;

You multiply before my eyes,
As manifold as pain or error,
Sit in the fixed mind and devise
Your own malign loose shapes of terror:

I see them crouching everywhere,
May yet become their myriad hands,
Innumerable mouths that dare,
Unformed, to glut their own demands.

Illusive many! you are one—
Privation of the saving thought;
Dreading what still must be, I run
Lost to what is for what is not.

AFTER A TIME

After a time, all losses are the same.
One more thing lost is one thing less to lose;
And we go stripped at last the way we came.

Though we shall probe, time and again, our shame,
Who lack the wit to keep or to refuse,
After a time, all losses are the same.

No wit, no luck can beat a losing game;
Good fortune is a reassuring ruse,
And we go stripped at last the way we came.

Rage as we will for what we think to claim,
Nothing so much as this bare thought subdues:
After a time, all losses are the same.

The sense of treachery—the want, the blame—
Goes in the end, whether or not we choose,
And we go stripped at last the way we came.

So we, who would go raging, will go tame
When what we have we can no longer use:
After a time, all losses are the same;
And we go stripped at last the way we came.

UNDER THIS LINTEL

in memory of Yvor Winters

Albeid that thow wer never so stout,
Undir this lyntell sall thow lowt;
Thair is nane uther way besyd.
                    —William Dunbar

This is the stone, my pride;
Under this you must bend,
Under this you must break;
Here I shall, though not mend,
Not want you at my side,
Do nothing for your sake.

This is the stone: a place
That is no place, my pride—
Only a mark at last.
You will not here provide:
This one pre-empted space
Is mine, my one holdfast.

Under this lintel stone,
Your limit, my support,
I shall not, loath to cross,
To fear no more this thwart
Shadow, confront your own
With this: The most is loss.

LATE

At different moments, they both crossed different bridges
over the lake, and saw swans folded, dark-white cyphers
on the white water, in an immortal dream.
                                        —Elizabeth Bowen

Dusk and cold distances in Regent's Park:
Air like a breath from clay, and, not yet dark,

The terraces withdrawn; this freeze will hold.
This is the height of winter—a bronze cold;

The trees soar stiffly up; and, on the lake,
Where still the thin ice segments tap and break,

In frozen woody brown, the islands stand;
Footbridges join the islands to the land.

But steering through dark channels under these,
Slow and indignant, moving at their ease,

Athwart the present in the hearts of men,
Insolent as the past, the swans again!

As once at Coole—great sudden forms in flight!—
So these, suave apparitions, hold the sight.

They haunted you, haunt us, cross and recross—
Calm emblems of unprecedented loss!

They pass, unlike, in empty, pure disdain;
And yet, superb enigmas, they remain.

For, won to that which stays the while it goes,
You won from them an intricate repose,

Drew season out of season to this lull
That keeps them here. Now, inexhaustible,

Their necks outthrust or arched like ancient prows,
They start in prescient flight, or, folded, drowse,

Or nest, or cleave the lake in passionate dream;
They hold the river where they paused midstream,

Then, late, above the marsh forever climb:
For you have mastered them that master time.

A FEW QUIET DAYS

Now for a time commend
Your days to quietness.
These, too, will have an end
But shall be yours no less.

If busy eyes pursue,
Practice an old deceit:
Be sure they see in you
Idleness and retreat.

And if you seem to sleep,
Then be content to seem;
Let stillness grow so deep
That none, in this extreme

Of instants motionless,
Suspects the active part,
The running wakefulness
That stays the mind and heart:

True mentor of your art.

THE NARROW HOUSE

in angusta domo

In anguish, in the narrow house,
I heard the reeling fly, the mouse,
The living with the dead carouse
    In the narrow house.

Then in the close, exhausted air
I smelled corruption; no one there
Could see the past's dead hand, or care
    For the narrow house.

I touched love's soft, dissolving face,
Sensed the anonymous disgrace
Of those cast out, who had no place
    But the narrow house.

I said, though with averted eyes,
These are as brief and dense as flies—
God pity! but who stays here dies
    In a narrow house.

Even the mind then acquiesced
To seek the ground of love and rest
And willingly was dispossessed
    Of the narrow house.

So love was the recurring dread
Of the abyss of loss instead,
From which same fear the heart had fled
    From the narrow house.

Unrest turned a bare, fugitive
Existence, which at most could give
Change from the change in which they live
   In the narrow house.

Who, looking back, can bear escape?
Their presences, still grieving, gape;
Who shuns their anguish takes their shape
   In a narrow house.

Who sees them once as not unique
But kindred creatures still must seek
Lost gentleness, gently to speak
   For the narrow house.

THE FIRST STEP

for Joseph DeRoche

The last step is the first.
And so I have descended
(Being of single mind)
Through fifteen narrow years,
And known what I intended
But not what I should find.
The downward flight, reversed,
As I look back in dread,
Ascends and disappears
In shadow overhead.

What will the next step be?
It should have been the climb,
The ardent foot and hand
Seeking the laurel rood.
But I have come in time
To know that where I stand
Is not the place where he,
Bernard, or some lost guide
Who led me here, had stood,
Stripped of his lusts and pride.

This figure of the stair,
Being a monk's design,
Having a monk's intent
Of purging self-regard,
I must at last resign
(God knows, some monks repent!)
As neither here nor there.
The self unsatisfied

Is what I find, Bernard,
Not God; nothing but pride.

How does it help, sweet saint,
To know our wretchedness,
When there's no going back?
How does it help to know
By heart how comfortless
We are, how much we lack,
And what we fear? The taint
Of death, of broken meat,
I've tasted, too, and oh
How cold the food I eat!

How does it help to see
How sick at heart we are
Or find out where we erred?
I see both whence I came
And where I am, how far
I've drifted who preferred
My own fool vagrancy:
If knowing this, I go
My own way all the same,
How does it help to know?

I NEED MORE LIGHT

I hurt who hurts me not to be alone,
And then, alone, I hate the hurt I give;
I need more light, or to be made of stone.

I need to shape a life less fugitive,
Where something will stay put and stay my hands,
For no one can run out of life and live.

I need a steadfast heart, a heart that stands
Still as the still eye of the storm is still.
Turbulent child, what next? what new demands?

Nothing can dry your eyes, nothing fulfill
Your needs, inexorable as your grief,
Grievous as death. You are as dark and shrill

As the wind surging, tumbling, I your leaf,
Your sport, your mere plaything. I need, I need
More than your hurt, your hate, your disbelief.

I need the darkness in you to recede
A little, for I need, not better sight
Nor to be made of stone. I need more light.

OUT OF WORK, OUT OF TOUCH, OUT OF SORTS

Dupont Circle, Washington, D.C.

Already past mid-June,
And something should be done;
I sit all afternoon,
Feeling both out of touch
And out of sorts, and sun
Myself on a bench near
The fountain; there's not much
On a temporary basis
That I know how to do.
What will my coming here,
Summer spent, amount to?
One of my wild goose chases?

Carved on the fountain's base
Are the bare name and dates
Of the man whom this place,
A wreath of water, leaf,
And stone, commemorates;
Wind, Ocean, Stars as three
Figures in high relief
Circle the shaft. The hand
That undertook his story
For the passersby and me
Lost it in allegory—
The thing is much too grand.

The passersby pass by.
They look instead at me
Or those they meet, as I

At them. The admiral
Himself would no doubt be
Surprised, were he to pass
His lost memorial.
The mere water striking
The bowl's edges, the trim
Bushes, young leaves and grass,
Which also might please him,
Are much more to our liking.

All winter long this scene—
The walks, spokes of a wheel,
The civil white and green
Of everyday concerns,
The Circle like a reel
On which the gigantic thread
Of traffic sings and turns,
The staid fountain's commotion—
Turned in my mind and brought,
For every move that led
Forward, a quicker thought
In steady countermotion.

Images of the past
Simplify as they grow
Centrifugal and vast:
The days all run together;
The long, eccentric snow
Of being somewhere else

Falls through perfect weather;
Starlings once seen flying
In pairs, wing guiding wing
With the wild, irregular pulse
Of love in late-found spring,
Circle together, crying.

Nothing is quite like that—
This city, least of all;
I think of the times I've sat
In the shadow of events
Faceless, impersonal.
What stone colossus' hands
Altered the private sense
Of how much one can master?
That others also grope
Shapes what one understands,
Facing the downward slope
Of a decade's near-disaster.

I almost learned, for once,
To take things as they come;
So now the eye confronts,
Not the past spun beyond
Itself, but the humdrum
Comings and goings of such
As momently respond
Only to what is living,
Momently changed within.

I sense, almost in touch,
But minding what has been,
The present's gift of giving.

THE SUMMER LEAVES

nothing unscathed. Desires,
once tender stalks, grow brittle;
the first and clear-eyed dew
that clung thereto
expires.

The summer leaves—the trees'
dense growth—that, dying little
by little, turn red, brown,
go down and down
and these

still leaves long winds will shake
and put me on my mettle—
here, rusted as dead blood,
there, bright, my good—
both make

the most of light. And then,
as, torn, the leaves resettle,
and the heart, ravaged, grieves,
the summer leaves
again.

BELONGINGS

Nothing about the first abandonment
In which the loose leaves lost their grip and slid
Dumbly, obliquely down to lie for days
On porches, lawns, and walks or skid along
The streets indifferently—nothing about
The way the birds took off, black against white
White skies, or day slumped and the dismal ground
Beneath her faded out—unsettled her.
It was all routine. It was the backward look
Of certain hours and how the warm air lagged,
The wind wavered and stopped, the leaves hung on;
It was the unexpectedly dense light
Late afternoons like hoarded gold, holding
For her the old effects, the diverse trash
Of other hours, belongings held too long
Because they once had served, although they served
No longer, and to which she thus belonged.
Had she not, summerlong, resolved that all
Loved grievous things, though they should prove the whole,
Would be, once and for all, swept up and out?
So, when a fine, cold, desolating rain
And wind, needling and nudging her, began,
She felt the comfort of their empty hands.
Had she believed that wind cried or that rain
Was querulous, she might have heard in them
A general reluctance to be done.
But, as it was, it was the usual drift
Of all expendables, reminding her
What she belonged to, what belonged to her.

THE YEARS

Then came the year of fires.
The burnings always took—
Because of the freezing nights,
The way the sick elms shook—
The form of lost desires,
Of purification rites.

Within the fires there stirred
The years, the years of rage.
Could fire, then, not exhaust
What tears could not assuage?
The flames' tongues all demurred.
And then, to be sure to be lost,

Within myself I knelt
To the venomous flames as they rose
From the dreamless dark and stilled
The years of unrepose
And unrelease; I felt
Tired to the bone and chilled.

What year, which I begin,
With the dying sound in my ears
Of the fire's rattle and hiss,
Afraid, because of the years,
Not to be looking in
And looking out, is this?

THE EUMENIDES

Come, my pretty drudges, kneel,
Come, black drudges, wound and heal,
Come, black judges!
         Who had called
I knew well and stood appalled;
Then I heard the cry begin,
Come, black judges! far within—
Head and heart, and all, engrossed
By this sad, malignant ghost.
I, who now for years had fled,
Turned in slow fatigue and dread
To confront them all at last,
Ghost and furies, furious past:
There the ghost wept, fixed in pain,
Young but evil, half-insane
With a malice unappeased—
Head and heart, and all, diseased.
At her side the furies knelt.
Old, but they seemed gentler, svelte,
Undulating creatures there
—Flowing bodies, serpent hair—
And those gently pulsing wings:
Beautiful nocturnal things.
Then they showed, in mild surprise,
Their blood-filled and -stiffened eyes;
And I knew them as they were:
Once the Keres, strong in her—
Ghosts but dark bacilli, thence
Blind and blinding pestilence,
Rage, blood-hunting, a disease—

Sorrow turned Erinyes,
Bound to sanction crime for crime—
Grief inscrutable as time.

Then I wept for me, for her,
What we are and what we were;
And the furies' wings grew white,
Star-informed, hair heaven-bright;
Furious voices, eyes were quiet.
They that lived with outrage, riot,
Anger, hate, fear, murderous madness,
Turned, embracing gladness, sadness.
They were knowledge and, as such,
Blessèd by compassion's touch.
And I found myself again
Turning toward the world of men.

AN ORDINARY SUNDAY MORNING
IN IOWA CITY
for Michael Van Walleghen

All Sundays tend to be a little blank.
But here, without *The New York Times* to hide
Behind, to clutter the rooms, the mind with news
And make our fatuous Sundays plausible,
The early stillness, sunny or sunless or
More often middling, unmysterious,
Suggests mere hours distended, lolling, dull.
One sleeps too late on purpose, wakes to find
That what one feared, the dumbness at the heart
Of everything, afflicts the morning air.

One phones, but no one's there or nothing doing.

From my fourth-story window I can see
People on their way to church, praise God—
It means a little movement down below.
The streets are wider than they were all week.
Clothed in their Sunday habits, long and loose,
Silence and grayness slide through the veiled sky.

The day has nothing up its sleeve but rain.

A SMALL RIVER IN IOWA AND THE WIDE WORLD

July, late afternoon. I sit alone
And look at only water; the still river,
On which the homely bridge's arches cast
Three perfect oval mirrors less than a stone
May break and break the stillness, soon will shiver
With life, be lost, imperfect as the past.

What of imperfect love? which wears perfection
A day an hour a moment—a moment's wonder
That fails as morning's dew, as mornings do.
This small river's a good place for reflection:
Its little hour, before the sun goes under,
Begins to change. Then what of me? of you?

We talked that other hour of love, but not
Of mine, of yours for someone else. Now all
This afternoon I've thought of love and you,
Who are not here. The wide world makes a knot
Of spirit bones flesh blood dark love loss gall.
And yet the grass, come night, is laced with dew.

This river, quick with carp as thick as mud,
Is a cool place where idlers like to pass
An hour or two and fish or contemplate
The fire-swept wings of the blackbirds, the flood
Of feelings that their shadows on the grass
Give rise to, as the day flames down, turns slate.

And O how fleeting the seasons are, how on
And on they stream! Do you not feel with me
How cold the grass is? Will you never fear
This chilling, failing light? The sun is gone.
The river's glassy now. Do you not see
How still it is again? You are not here.

No matter. All this will soon be done.
And I shall leave for good this riverbank—
Sleek carp the redwings this close-knotted earth
The bridge its mirrors the hours will be as one.
Before the air darkens and goes blank,
Where will the world have brought me? What was it worth?

When all these that were shimmer, shadow, or gloss
Are far from here, shall I remember then
The river as a world wide as wonder
That flows, entwines continuous change with loss?
Having once been, shall I be once again
Aware of earth's both excellence and plunder?

THE PASSING OF EDEN
Pomona, California
for Glen Epstein

There are foxes on this hill,
friend, and rattlesnakes. But deer
also wander dreamily
among the palms, persimmons,
and cypresses and appear
at Kellogg Mansion to browse
on the lawn and even come
down at night when no one's near
to the dreamless beds below
where roses on roses bloom,
filling the night air, all year
round; but which, for some time past,
thieves or, not prizing the long
stems, perhaps vandals—from mere
meanness was the common view—
have been ripping off. I read
today it's becoming clear
who the culprits are. But oh
the deer—I saw one close by
but fugitive, without peer
for remoteness—know nothing
of the passing of Eden
or the price of roses here.
Still, whenever I linger
absently in the garden
now, I wonder, will I hear
the whispers of hooves, as light
as sighs, among the roses?
What can we do when the deer,

half-visions all day, steal down
at night from the hill and eat
the roses and disappear?

SOMETHING TO BE SAID

They who lie down each night with gloom,
Who listen to the false alarms
Of crones who give the flesh no room,
Who see no grace in glitter, joy, or bloom
And do without it,

Keep their potato patches hoed;
But there are some things safety harms,
And order, too, will discommode
When all the roses miles around explode—
No doubt about it.

There may be something to be said
For saying over: Fill your arms
With roses; in your last worst bed
You will be neither grieved nor comforted.
Be quick about it.

TEACHER

Once
I said something
I've forgotten what

so well

twenty-three heads
together
forgot themselves

bent over their notebooks
set it down
and looked up

expectantly

that was all
but it gave me
pause

I wonder what it was

MESSAGE

Dear Sister, where are you? You never knew
What time and time's remorselessness could do.
How can you think your silence is complete?
The heart fails, but pitiless years repeat
The clear, unspeakable malice of the dead;
The grief you came to was the past you fled.

RAILROADS

run through
            my life
                        like
fire
            cats and
                        cars.
The father
            of the man
                        to whom I
dedicated
            my first book
                        was a railroad man.
My former
            lover's father
                        a Wobbly
who loved
            Raymond Chandler's novels
                        and died in an
accident
            (like
                        almost
everyone else)
            was a railroad man.
                        My mother's
sister's
            husband
                        was a railroad man
The last time
            I saw
                        her

(three weeks
                    before her sister
                                        youngest
in a family of nine
                    died in an
                                        accident
of the blood
                    cells
                                        that kept
multiplying
                    white
                                        when she needed
an addition of
                    red
                                        a terrible
mistake
                    excessive
                                        as life
which is
                    death)
                                        was the last time I saw him.

When I
                    was a
                                        little girl
we lived
                    by the railroad tracks
                                        in South
Bottoms
                    Sioux City Iowa.

                                    Whenever
mother
                    happened not
                                    to be home
the hoboes
                    we
                                    my sister and I
fed!

                    Two
                                    of the best
painters
                    I ever knew
                                    are railroad men
and whenever I find
                    myself on a train
                                    I write
and write
                    and
                                    write and
you
                    Otis
                                    whom I keep
track of
                    (as best I can)
                                        are living
on Railroad Avenue.
                    That beats
                                    all.

SHE

gave me life
    what a hell
        on wheels she was
            but
drive!
    indestructible (almost)
                down
        snaky
           pitchdark
        highways blind
curves
    hairpin
turns
    the chances she took
        (if you wouldn't dim your lights
neither would she)
        a good
           head on her shoulders
quick reflexes
      but no
        spare or
        no brakes at all
           a welter of
signals and signs
      signifying
        something to
someone else
      (too hell-
      bent

to look)
stopping
only to refuel
and then to drive on like mad to make up
for lost time
(losing
the way) and
always in a storm of
rage   laughter
torrents of
words and
wit
curses and
tears
(or as the song on the jukebox goes
"if you think I laugh too loud
you should hear me
cry")
oh
the collisions
the wrecks as if
driven
by some demon
lover of
go and
find and
get
(but what?
not money)

the good die
young so
she kept going
an unforgettable
occurrence
tearing through
at 3 a.m.
dangerous
to ignore
no apparition
but a dream
awakened
of longing in all directions
and the roads
all open
In the determined
course of her life
she gave as
good
as she got
and
here I am

SECOND THOUGHTS

My mother used to say. "I'll beat the living Jesus out of you."
She almost did.
And so, whenever I was really sick to death, I used to say:
"I'll hurt them where they live."
I tried and tried and tried until I almost died,
But never really could.
And so, one night I wrote a poem about her and her drive
With almost love.
I wrote: Maybe she really didn't even mean it, after all.
I wrote: Maybe I'm just like her, no matter what.
I wrote: She gave me life and could not take it back.

THE UNPROFITABLE SERVANT

Now, when I wake to darkness, if I think
What I shall come to be, I think of all
I have not been; I have myself to thank.
I thank myself: For we are all as ill
As he; unprofitable, holding out
And hiding out, we cannot quite come through.
Devouring God, it is ourselves we eat.
We cannot, as we would, say thee and thou,
Cast utterly out like him. We cannot help it.

TO A BOTTLE

prithee, not smile, or smile more inly
—Robert Herrick, *Farewell to Sack*

At first, while I was sober, friend,
Thinking the night would never end,
You sat there loaded. Spirits high,
You seemed all smiles and glow, so I
Smiled back at you. And all was well,
But as my spirits rose, yours fell.
Now I am loaded. You sit there
With a cold-sober, empty stare.
Why did I ever take a shine
To you? Your grin is gone. So's mine.

This is not a bottle.

FOR TENDER STALKES

*for Harry Duncan, who introduced me
to Ralegh's fragment "The Ocean to Cynthia"*

1.

If any truly are not haunted
By lost names with familiar faces
That come unsummoned and unwanted,
Let them repeat love's commonplaces.

But when we met and when we parted,
We made no promises, we set
No day; the light but heavyhearted
Remember how much they forget.

Thus we have had to pay, and dearly,
For so unpromising a love,
As deep a pact, denied, unspoken,
As any have been guilty of;
And worse, our sealed lips told how nearly
It touched us that it might be broken.

2.

All winter long I thought: Together,
Our own June will dispel this other
Relentless, black, and tossing weather,
This ill-feeling toward one another.

Absence, the change, the morbid chill,
As some huge and preposterous snow,
Stiffened your tender care until
It broke. You thought it better so.

The fierce contagion of that thought
Has worsened me and altered mine:
Yes, it is better so. The best
Thing I could do was to resign
A love so wasting and distraught,
It let me neither work nor rest.

3.

The bitter waste, the long distraction,
The graveclod heaviness within,
Passion, become a numbed inaction,
Ravage both love and discipline.

Catullus brought to passion skill,
To anger wit, and eased and mended
His bruised heart and his baffled will
In waking song, when love was ended.

Make honey of your gall, my sorrow,
And choice of this necessity;
Prefer your indigence nor borrow
From vacant love new destitution:
Make unlike songs, secure but free.
Let this be your full restitution.

4.

Do but consider how you went
To prove another's worth, and more

Than once; returned, restlessness spent,
To find what you were looking for.

What did I do then? Did I scold?
Refuse you? Did I play your game?
Who reasoned, reconciled, consoled?
On whom then did we place the blame?

Who's constant? You? because you go
But always come back? at your leisure.
Or I? who changed to let you know
That love, not I, would be the same,
And thus was self-betrayed: Your game.
I go; I'll come back. At my pleasure.

5.

When heaven was the haven-portal,
To restless flesh the ground of rest
And love, when mortals were immortal,
The loved, won hand grew still, but for the best.

Now the heart stops and stops forever.
We cannot keep the things we keep.
And so, willful, we quickly sever
Ourselves from what we love, toward sleep.

Better that we see clearly, truly,
Although it cost us all but all
And time be lost in knowing this,

Than that death should possess us, call
And call, although it does. Unruly,
We're not for hate or cowardice.

6.

Petrarch in secret feared he must
Die three deaths and die with the third
Indeed, to all the world be dust,
Even dust, his art; he grieved: Love heard.

Love, who as All knew why, knows not
How this can be, who consecrated
This fearful loving that begot
The dread of being uncreated.

Our bodies are the graves and churches
Where being near unbeing dwells;
Love meets here what it likes, dislikes,
Bends down, of two minds, strokes and strikes,
Finds in the good for which it searches
The dark it gathers and dispels.

7.

Sleepless, I think: how I should sleep
Cradled, as once, all night and eased
Of all the anguish that I keep
Pent up, alone, awake, diseased.

But then I think how restless I
Have been with love, how I would toss

And turn, would, though with love, still lie
Alone, possessed by an unknown loss.

It is not lack of love that left us
Sad as Simonides, whose sadness
Never embraced this unloved madness
That let the thought of such loss war
With having, which grief has bereft us
Of peace. But that is where we are.

8.

A deadly time for all:
Dangerous streets, curbs, walks;
The sky, enormous pall,
Spells death for tender stalks.

In all that color, darkness;
Their blooms were all death's-heads;
Their leaves hid winter's starkness;
Their green couch, graveyard beds.

For tender stalks, as lovers
Naked, shaken, afraid,
As time alone discovers,
Bend when the first storm hovers,
Breaks: this slight reed was made
For tender stalks as lovers.

TO AN ARCHAEOLOGIST SOME YEARS HENCE
for M.H.J.

Our error was
we made free
with one another.

But crowds of frightened
women jeering at
children with such
poise under pressure
phenomenal aim
learning derided
the pack the loners
North Beach Venice
West the Village
swarming with cops
sickness misery
blight
or everything new
money bleak lawns
cosmetics for corpses
stuffed like birds
a time-buying world
of small conveniences
enormous discomforts
and cars cars
the Bay lost
the old view gone
in a nation so
dedicated

told us what we hated
but had to see.

In the litter of shattered
windows and lives
houses divided
in the trash
the ashes of books
you can read
the crystal nights
that at least made
the whole mess clear.

THE SUMMER THAT NEVER WAS

1. The Summer in Early Spring
    to the memory of Martin Luther King, Jr.

The King is dead.
The summer came in early spring this year.
The King is dead.
How timeless do we have to be
to be able to tell one another the time of day?
The King is dead.
The morning glories, which have not yet arrived,
are bursting with life,
but the King is dead.
Who would have dreamed
on an April day bursting with life
of the dream exploding in his dreaming head?
The King is dead.
The morning glories,
which have not yet arrived bursting with life and dying,
are as blue as the sky has to be to be heaven,
but the King is dead.
The whole world wept last night.
The King was dead.
The whole world is blue today.
The King is dead.
How can we tell,
on this summer day bursting
and dying in early spring,
the time of year
when the King is dead?
How can there be, in such a time, on such a day,

the thought of spring or summer?
The King is dead.
Heaven today is to be able to tell one another,
not the time of year, but the time of day.
For the King is dead.
May the seeds of the heavenly blue morning glories survive.
Will the King and his dream of a heavenly day,
in the summer that never was,
arrive?

Is the King alive?

What is the color of sorrow?

2.   The Summer That Only Is
        near Macon, Missouri

This is Still-Hildreth,
a private hospital going to seed.
When I arrived
in August, in the dark,
after four months of dead-white nights,
I saw few patients;
the rest were gone or too far gone to go.
What greeted me
was Still-Hildreth,
a hospital gone or going to seed.
I greeted it
as one who may or may not stay.

The summer that is is worse than uninspired.
I sit alone
in a cell-sized room, wondering what I desired,
desire; or walk around
unsure and more than tired
of no firm ground—
the future as the present blown
apart—not least of all
the small
and inward peace that has almost expired.

Still-Hildreth,
whose grounds are pleasant for strolling,
being large and serene,
has a short, straight driveway
that circles in front of the entrance doors
and meanders in back
around an untidy pond;
there, wildflowers, especially the wild carrot,
are everywhere.
Today I saw from the mute concert room
the useless tennis courts, the lawn around
well groomed and green.
Beyond are picnic tables, benches, and folding chairs,
deserted now,
and one small table
where I come to write, to find some peace.

The summer has never been like this before,
or not for me,

so personal, impersonal a war.
Who can escape, turned outside in,
the hawk within and the unknown predator?
whose discipline
is death, whose love must be
a love of hatred, crud,
greed, blood,
and the maimed lives and loves that cry: No more.

Still-Hildreth, a block of bricks
that looks
like nothing that could ever go to seed,
once an academy for the glory of war
with a still splendid staircase
made curious with iron tendrils and stone trefoil forms
like clover leaves without the luck
and rich with rails of brass and flowerlike brass motifs
is dying
from end to end
of unused massive space.

The summer that only was has gone to seed,
whether or not
Still-Hildreth goes, whether it meets my need,
which is to know what I
should do and how then to proceed.
I wonder why
when something has been shot
to hell, it is my hell
as well.
Though clearly it cannot be, it is indeed.

3.   The Indian Pipe
      to the memory of Robert F. Kennedy

St. Francis, all the little flowers are dead.
                Autumn has come.
The summer that never was has somehow fled.
        The tiny temple bells,
their rich, greathearted leaves, blood-red,
        the heartfelt knells
    that told our fears are dumb;
    spring beauties, red and gold,
                are cold,
and every tender stalk has lost its head.

    Where are June's copious beds?
Can the full season, just rose, be denied?
        stripped of their flowers,
            their due rose hours,
                war-torn,
    dead-white where something died?
        What is this horn
    of death-filled autumn reds?

    June's gentle first increase,
            our budding peace,
whose thorny presence left only his own seed,
        burst with his shattered head
                bright red,
        while the hell-blooms of war,
flesh roses that explode and bleed,
            are as before.

Speak of untimely dead, Francis, untoward
silence, all the abhorred
unnatural voids, the blank
pages, missed connections, the horde
of things gone rank
too soon, the seeds that never thrived
deprived
by chance—of how much cannot be restored.

Speak of our festered ghettos;
our lily-white
suburbs; luxurious estates,
their filigree,
but iron bars on windows,
their high rails, spikes on posts and gates
—all barricades—a disguised incivility.
Speak of the abyss
and why we have come to this:
the bloom
of our white mushroom,
like an enormous, spreading saprophyte,
our ghostly Indian pipe, feeding on death, not light.

BEGGING FOR CHANGE

His face a volcano
erupting
a molten glass of despair—
just another bum on Boylston,
with a damaged, dressed,
and heavily bandaged leg,
his trivial badge of survival
begging for change.

I admit I gave him
reluctantly
a little change—
as once in a while
I do, changing
nothing—besides
he was cheerful—
and, anyway,
trivial to whom?

Also, I know
what it is to be
truly
hard up
for a drink.

THE WILLOWS IN WINTER IN THE BOSTON PUBLIC GARDEN

In the sun's white
  In a morning ambience of milky blue,
  Fresh snow upon the ground
  And all around
  All sorts of trees stand out
  With a new
  Spare
  And alert air;
  But from a nearby path,
  The willows with straight, yellow, chopped-off hair
  Look, to the altered view,
  For all the world as if they did not care
  How many sweeping winters they
  Have looked this way,
  Or how they have appeared before, their fine
  Long tremulous veils of hair
  Blown all one way or hanging heavy there,
  Or how much longer now they have to stay.

In diffused light
  In the middle distance in late afternoon,
  The sky beyond as candid as the snow,
  A show-through ochre haze
  With, here and there, a thick deep ochre line,
  As if the willows' presence truly seen
  Were but a fine
  Discretion,
  A matter of distinguishing degrees,
  The differences between

A slight
Absence and a light
Presence
Or a deep
And deeper shades of golds,
Their interplays,
Interstices
Of lights and willow-shadows, opacities and sheens.

And at night
  Close and starkly from below,
  But with an upward gaze,
  As within
  The dizzy soul begins its own ascent, without
  The clear-eyed wide repose it seeks,
  Toward those high
  Severe exhilarating peaks,
  Marvels of unease,
  Surprise, astonishment, and awe,
  The eye,
  Through thick and thin in black and naked lines,
  Against that far-out crystal bowl the sky,
  Beholds
  A crazy any-which-way maze
  Become a sharp and kind of counter outward daze,
  As if the stars sprang from a stunning blow,
  Startling the winter night
  And dazzling snow.

FINDING A WAY

This, it may be, is one way
That the interstices
Of sound and thought and feeling
When all else is unease
Might be given continuous play.
We would possess
The inexpressibly near,
Stealing
From distance, by formal means,
The unclear,
Immediate, fugitive in-betweens.

This may be one way: for here
The indistinct footfalls
The always half-heard
Coming and goings of the unknown
Will strike the ear.
The intervals
Will be silence speaking, finding
The word
That evokes what might have fled
Reminding
The spirit to listen for the unsaid.

FINDING OURSELVES AND OTHERS
for H. E. and G. M.

Are we not all both
One and many? slow
To find how opaque
We are and how loath
To be so,
       to wake

From the dream of one's
Self, live with the rifts
Of chance, the welter
That momently runs
And shifts
       from shelter

To change and unease
And find, not merely
Our own manifold
Ambiguities,
But clearly
       a hold

On common weather:
O replete with suns,
Freeze, downpours, lulls, blast!
(In this, together!)
None's
       so sure at last

Or so much his own
As to disregard

The rest, or how dis-
Mal we are alone.
But how hard
            it is

To be open, bear
The differences of
Others, or try to.
If we can, a rare
And radiant love,
Now and then, breaks through.

GO

Go, little book: I cannot say
Whether I'd have you leave or stay,
Since you're so ready now to try
Your luck with every passerby.
But if I say (and mean it too),
It is a whorish thing to do,
A loveless promiscuity,
To go in every company,
I see in you no such success
As would confirm your restlessness:
How will you catch the casual eye?
You're both too haughty and too shy—
Too plain besides, poor silly goose,
Ever to play it fast and loose.
But go! Better to learn the worst
(As I have taught you from the first)
Than to delude yourself. I give
Here my best life; but you must live
By other hands than those that gave.
I gave. I cannot also save.

NOTES

BEFORE YOU ENTER: Written in 1971, this was the prefatory poem in the manuscript Davis assembled in 1995, *Yes Is a Very Big Word*. We print the first of several versions.

INSIGHTS is the title Davis gave to her compilation of epigrams, to which she kept adding (and from which she sometimes cut). In her 1998 chapbook and her 1995 manuscript, the title is "Looking In and Looking Out."

THE FIRST STEP: *Non dico ut te facias quod non se, sed ut attendas quid es, quia vere miser es, et sic disces misereri, qui hoc aliter scire non potes.* —Bernard of Clairvaux
("I do not say that you should make of yourself what you are not but that you heed what you are, for you are truly wretched, and so may understand the wretchedness of others: there is no other way.") [author's note]

A SMALL RIVER IN IOWA AND THE WIDE WORLD: The last and shortest of several versions, this is the one Davis included in her 1995 manuscript. The first, titled "The Wide World," was somewhat longer, and Davis made many attempts to add new sections between 1973 and 1977.

THE PASSING OF EDEN: See pp. 199-200 for Davis's notes on revisions of this poem.

MESSAGE: A late revision of "To C.D.M.," which appeared as the first of several "Insights" in *Quest for Reality*, ed. Winters and Fields (1969). Although versions of both "Message" and "To a

Bottle" appear in a 1956 notebook, the first was not published in its current form, and the second was not published at all, until 1998.

RAILROADS: The earliest and shortest of several versions of this poem, probably a first draft. Some small corrections that appear in the next two versions of the poem have been added here.

FOR TENDER STALKES is the last unfinished line of Ralegh's fragment "The Ocean to Cynthia." [author's note] In a 1996 letter to Donald Justice, Davis wrote: "The structure is the disjunctive syllogism (if, but, so)——however, sometimes, in the second quatrain … instead of being opposites, they are merely contrasts or even intensives—and the tetrameters, especially with all those feminine endings (I hoped) would give it a lyrical quality: logic with song. I also liked the idea of ending the sonnets with a trim trimeter."

The first sonnets for this sequence were written in 1964; Davis kept writing them until at least 1970. In her 1995 manuscript, she omitted seven of the fifteen published in 1971, but added two more. This collection prints the eight that appear in both sequences.

TO AN ARCHAEOLOGIST SOME YEARS HENCE is the second section of "Yes Is a Very Big Word," a three-part poem begun in 1963, with a coda added in 1968.

BEGGING FOR CHANGE is the second section of *"the pure products of America,"* an eight-part sequence written in 1974–75.

THE WILLOWS IN WINTER IN THE PUBLIC GARDEN: Although it was not included in Davis's 1995 manuscript, this poem, begun in

1974, was the final poem in an undated compilation of poems titled simply "Poems."

FINDING A WAY appears in a notebook with a 1998 date, though it is apparently a revision of an earlier poem.

FINDING OURSELVES AND OTHERS: Probably the last poem Davis began and finished (in 1993-94), and (as she says in a letter to Nancy and Harry Duncan) the first she had written in seventeen years. This poem replaced an earlier sixth section of "Seven Types of Clarity," a seven-part poem that was published in *The Southern Review* but is not included in this collection.

GO: As "Nescis, Heu, Nescis," this is the final poem in "The Leaves," the first pamphlet Davis printed. As "Go," it is also the final poem in the 1995 manuscript.

INTERVIEW WITH MARIE PELLETIER

In March of 2014, Unsung Masters contacted Marie Pelletier, Catherine Breese Davis' companion for many years, to ask if she'd be interested in being interviewed for this book. The interview was conducted by Martin Rock and Kevin Prufer via email between August 17, 2014 and April 23, 2015, then shaped and edited in the months that followed. In October, 2014, Martha Collins and Kevin Prufer also visited Marie Pelletier in Massachusetts, where they looked through many of Catherine Davis' papers. These included notebooks of careful drafts of poems, journals, pamphlets, letters, and a leatherette book of "world poetry" meticulously handwritten by Catherine's father, all carefully stored in several boxes. Photographs of some of those items appear here, alongside photographs Marie Pelletier provided to us later, as we continued to work on this project.

—The Editors

Unsung Masters: Tell us about Catherine Breese Davis before you knew her. What do you know about her family and early life?

Marie Pelletier: Catherine was born in a Minneapolis hospital on October 24, 1924. Her parents were Robert and Louella Allen Davis, both of whom were young and poor. She grew up without her father, who committed an armed robbery with an unloaded gun; nevertheless he received a seven-year sentence and as a result Catherine never knew him. The marriage broke up after his release.

Catherine grew up thinking her name was Patricia Louella, Patsy-Lou. She detested the name, and only found out when she got her birth certificate, probably when she was enrolling in college, that her father had given her the name Catherine Breese Davis. She took the name immediately and with relief. Breese was her father's middle name, a family name no doubt—probably from his mother's side, as perhaps was the name Catherine.

Louella, Catherine's mother, was known for her lively personality. She never lacked for men and probably remarried without getting a divorce from her husband Robert—that was Catherine's guess. She was well-spoken but would go off on tears and used a profane blue vocabulary. I don't know what she did for work; Catherine never mentioned that to me. Later on, when Catherine was in high school, her mother managed a brothel for the man she lived with, who also owned a bar.

UM: That must have been a difficult environment for a child. Were there stories or events from Catherine's upbringing she shared with you?

MP: Catherine's mother couldn't have had an easy life raising two children without a husband. Catherine had an older sister, Charlotte, and when they were young, Catherine was placed in a foster home. The foster family's last name was de Wolff—I don't know the spelling, but I do know that Catherine was happy there, and went home on occasion. On one of these trips home, Catherine referred to Mrs. de Wolff as her mother, and when that happened, Louella ended the foster-care relationship. The two girls were sent to a Catholic convent boarding school for one year, but they were so wild and disobedient that the Sisters didn't allow them to return. I can just imagine—I know how unruly she could be.

At some point the family moved to Sioux City, Iowa, and that's where Catherine grew up and went to school until high school. Life was pretty rough and tumble there; they lived in a mixed working-class neighborhood which included Native Americans. The children all played and ran wild together.

She didn't talk much of that time and what I remember is that life was not pleasant. She did, however, enter a coffee brand naming contest with her mother. There was a new coffee line being marketed and the company wanted a name for the brand. She and her mother entered the contest and decided on the name MelloRoma. They didn't win. Good name though.

UM: What more can you tell us about Catherine's father? Did she ever give you any indication about what he was like?

MP: I really don't know much about her father except that he committed a robbery, as I mentioned, and was sent to jail in St. Cloud, Minnesota. He was sentenced to seven years and served either six or the full seven. He was able to write his mother and wife only once or twice a month, and he did write letters to both of them. He was in his twenties and Catherine was a year old or younger when he was sent to prison.

He read a great deal and was also a musician—I don't know which instrument—and played in the prison orchestra or band. They gave periodic concerts to which the families were invited. His letters are clear, well-constructed, grammatically correct, and fluid. He exhorts his wife in these letters to visit him—she was an irregular visitor, but in her defense the trip was a long one, over 60 miles, and she had two young children—and to write him more often. He would also offer advice as to the rearing of the children. The letters read as though he was just away from home on some kind of assignment, and not that he was in prison.

After her father was released he went to visit the family. Catherine wasn't there; it would be around the time she was

Robert B. Davis #1420
Friday, October 10, 193_

CENSORED

Dear Lue,

Received your letter, and while I had previously determined not to answer when you finally got around to writing, it was such an interesting letter that I find myself being reduced by your charm, as usual. I have two favors to ask of you, and though you will probably give no thought to either of them, still I cherish the __ hope that it will suit your pleasure to consider my petitions just once. The first is that you keep both the children in this Catholic school continuously for this last year. I doubt that you will do this, because I know just how sick you will get of paying $50.00 a month. But I'm sure it would be a fine thing for both of them if they could stay settled for a whole year. I am also sure that we will both benefit by having them stay there. This school will deliver our children to us when I am released exactly as we both want to see them, with good manners, a good foundation religiously, and with simple tastes. They will probably do more for their future good than both of us could do together. The second request has to do with your letters to me. I wish you would make an effort to write twice a month, and in your letters give me every detail concerning the care the children are getting. The babies are growing up in my absence and I'm not able to keep a mental picture of their development. I can remember them only as babies. I am overjoyed to hear that Charlotte is having piano lessons. There is no reason why Patsy could not begin now unless it is too

A letter written by Catherine's father from prison.

with the de Wolffs. He came to say good-bye, I guess, because he never came back and he gave Charlotte a ring; Catherine often mentioned the ring to me. She always regretted not seeing him—really a sorrow; she couldn't have remembered him since she was so young when he went to prison. His abandonment left a great blank in her life.

UM: When we last visited you showed us the beautiful book her father made, which we are grateful has not been destroyed. What can you tell us about this book?

MP: As a Christmas present to his wife, Catherine's father got a blank 8.5" x 11" notebook with a black leatherette cover and prepared a compendium of world poetry. It is over 200 pages; he writes only on the right-hand side. This was in 1930, the year before he was released from prison. It is extensive, painstakingly done and beautifully handwritten, with a foreword, a table of contents, and an index of first lines, and he went so far as to paginate it. He had design sense. He wrote with a nib pen, which occasionally gave him trouble. He does seem to cover the entire world of poetry, and then at the end of the notebook he writes his own Experiments—his poems—and it's clear from the last sonnet that he doesn't believe their marriage will last. At the end of the index of first lines he writes: "You have no idea what a helluva job this was! Amen."

UM: What more can you tell us about Catherine's relationship to her family?

MP: There was an incident with her mother. I don't remember the circumstances, but her mother beat her and Catherine wouldn't go to school because some of the bruises were evident. As a result, Catherine was truant, and the case went to court; at the court session Catherine asked if she could live with her aunt. The aunt agreed, and Catherine spent her high-school years with her aunt, her uncle and her two cousins—a boy named Adam, and I don't remember the female cousin's name. They were poor, but the uncle hunted and occasionally they had pheasant on the table. Her aunt took in laundry and accepted charity, which made Catherine feel ashamed, but her aunt made the point that it was the only choice they had and being embarrassed wasn't going to change their situation.

UM: What else do you know of Catherine's high-school years? Do you know if she'd yet begun writing? Was she involved in any other creative outlets?

MP: I assume she had been writing. I know that Catherine played the trumpet in high school and some big horn in the marching band, something like a tuba, which ruined her lip for the trumpet. And she had the first recognition of her homosexuality while she was there.

UM: Did she ever say anything about this realization, or how she felt about it?

MP: No, I don't think it came as a great revelation and I don't think it disturbed her much.

UM: In a letter to *The New Yorker* poetry editor Louise Bogan, Yvor Winters mentions that Catherine has a disability of some kind, though he doesn't name it. Can you tell us about that?

MP: Catherine had cerebral palsy, a very mild form, which was misdiagnosed as polio. As a result of the misdiagnosis a tendon was cut in her left ankle, ostensibly to help her walk, though it was not a help. She was properly diagnosed when she was going off to college and had to have a physical exam; the doctor recognized the symptoms. Catherine attributed her manic behavior to her cerebral palsy—she thought that it affected her neurologically, which no doubt was true, and it no doubt did exacerbate her manic side. Today she would be diagnosed as bipolar: she had highs and very black lows. You could tell when you saw her if she was in a black mood. Her look told the story.

UM: What can you tell us about the time immediately after Catherine finished high school?

Dear Lue,

In the preparation of this book I have tried to choose the best work of each poet with, however, some qualifications: I have used lyric poetry for the most part, because I thought you would prefer it to any other; I selected short poems wherever a choice was possible; and I have found it necessary to make some abridgements. I regret the necessity for these abridgements, for I am well aware that they cannot give you what the complete poem gives; yet I could not well include 102 stanzas of the "Rubaiyat," 43 sonnets of Mrs. Browning's masterpiece, 20 sonnets of Edna St. Vincent Millay's sequence, etc., and still keep this work within a single volume. There are many languages not represented here — Japanese, Arabian, Egyptian, Greek, Scandanavian, Russian, and so on — because I have thus far read no translations from these countries which compare favorably with the poetry I have selected. Obviously, then, this book falls far short of its somewhat ambiguous title; but I have wanted it to be a source of pleasure to you, not a text-book. Yet, limited in scope as it is, I have had to exercise some restraint. It was an effort for me to restrict myself to only a few poems from England and America, for I have so much beautiful poetry from both countries: thus, from England, Rupert Brooke could easily take half a volume, for of the many poets in my collection, he is still my favorite, not excepting even Shelley.

Regarding the work under the title "Experiments," I trust that you will be lenient in your judgement of my juvenile efforts. It seems almost a desecration to include them with the work of some of the greatest poets of all time, yet I'm sure you will understand that I do not rate myself a poet, but only wrote for you, and so that I might have something of my own to give you.

A note included in the manuscript of poetry Catherine's father compiled for her mother while in prison.

MP: When she came home from high school, her mother was running a brothel. I don't know how many women, but Catherine got to know them and joined in on their partying. There was a confrontation with her mother. Catherine may have been preparing to go off to the University of Minnesota (I'm not entirely sure) when she told her mother she that was a homosexual. Her mother drove her to the train station—the poem "She" relates the incident—and they never were in touch again. She did keep up with her sister Charlotte for as long as she could, but when I knew her she had lost touch with Charlotte and couldn't, although she tried, connect with her again.

UM: What do you know about her early experiences with poetry, including the poets with whom she studied?

MP: She went to the University of Minnesota, where she studied with Robert Penn Warren, and then during the war she moved to Chicago and attended the University of Chicago where she met J.V. Cunningham, who got her a fellowship to study with Yvor Winters at Stanford.

Perhaps before she attended the University of Chicago she worked in a government office, where she had a relationship with her supervisor, whose fiancé was off at war. She got to know the family, attended holiday dinners, and got acquainted with the middle class. Catherine at this point was a little like Edith Piaf, waif-like and unfamiliar with middle-class social mores, until she was introduced to them through this relationship. The relationship ended when the fiancé returned.

It was also in Chicago that Catherine got introduced to the homosexual sub-culture. At some point, she was also a page at the Newberry Library, but I'm not sure if this was while she was still in school. She loved libraries, and frequented them since she could rarely afford books. An interesting fact is that while she was at the University of Chicago, experiments in smashing the atom were going on under one of the sports stadiums. Neither the students nor the faculty knew of course; everyone was surprised when the news came out.

UM: You mention that Catherine studied at Stanford with Yvor Winters. Who else was at Stanford while she was there?

MP: Winters's students were Helen Pinkerton and Wes Trimpi, who weren't yet married, and Edgar Bowers, who had served in WWII. I don't remember the names of the others, but I know that Catherine became friendly with them and that they all had a merry time. Cunningham told Catherine

that the fellowship would be the only time in her life where she could enjoy a freedom she would never have again. He was right.

UM: What was her relationship with Winters like? And her other mentors? Did she talk about them with you?

MP: They were both central to her; they took her seriously, which gave her the foundation of approval and confidence any young poet needs, and she was grateful to them. I found this about Tate in one of the notebooks; she wrote this after she heard about his death:

> He was very good to me when I was young. I met him in 1947 at a Utah Writers Conference; he had deeply influenced me by then, and I had gone there (with Helene Draus) expressly to meet him. We corresponded for a while. He came to the Chicago campus in 1948 (with Louise Bogan that same spring) and I became acquainted with them both. I saw him again when he was invited to speak at Northeastern Missouri—we got drunk together that time, and I got into some trouble over it after he left. About four or five years ago I ran into him in Harvard Square, and I was so surprised I think I had little to say. No, it must have been longer ago than that—'72 or '73—because I remember I complained that Harper & Row had lost my ms. (in 1971) and I'm sure I wasn't working. He said "They're terrible people, Catherine!" He also called me a "faithless woman" because evidently I had promised in Kirksville to send him my ms. but had never done so (I hadn't remembered the promise).

We had gone to Harvard Square when we ran into Tate and Robert Fitzgerald. Tate was giving a talk at Harvard. Catherine went up to him to say hello.

UM: And what happened after Stanford?

MP: After Stanford she moved to New York City, where she wrote for *Cue* magazine—she really didn't like New York. There are NYC poems, as you know. It was there that she met Beth Nelson, who'd heard about Catherine from a friend. She made a trip to visit Catherine; they fell in love and she moved to Washington where Beth was living and working. Actually, they may have first moved to Baltimore because Beth was finishing her Ph.D. at Hopkins. Anyway, Beth got a job at Howard University teaching English. In DC, Catherine worked for the Education Department and didn't like it—she called them in the aggregate "the educationists." She worked near Dupont Circle and loved to visit the Phillips Collection and fell in love with Klee. The poem "Out of Work, Out of Touch, Out of Sorts" was written during this time.

She and Beth moved to Alexandria and rented a couple of Federal architecture houses there. She liked living there—it was a time when people could still afford it. She got interested in printing and bought a clamshell press and type—Bembo, an Italian face named after Cardinal Bembo. One of the features or peculiarities of this face is that the ascender height exceeds the cap height. How she managed a press, type, paper, printing, binding, I don't know, but she loved printing and when she got to Iowa she took typography courses with Harry Duncan and they

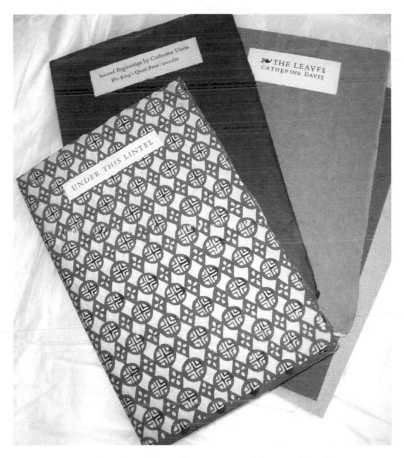

became friends. She printed one pamphlet under the imprint of Bembo Press and two (one with Harry Duncan) under the imprint of King's Quair Press. Beth and she bought a dog—a Basenji, which was originally an African hunting breed that doesn't bark so much as yodel. Beth sent her the dog as a present when Catherine was at Iowa, and she called him Phip. She eventually gave it to a loving family; her life in Iowa wasn't regular enough to keep a dog.

UM: Do you think this interest in the printing press came about solely because of Catherine's relationship to poetry, or was there some other reason that she became so involved with printing?

MP: No, she was interested in design, obviously. Who knows where it comes from? It's like poetry: who knows where that comes from? She took after her father perhaps—and her mother as well.

UM: Can you tell us more about Beth?

MP: Beth Nelson's father was a railroad man and was killed in a railroad accident. J.V. Cunningham's father also worked for the railroads, and Catherine's poem "Railroads" acknowledges that background.

She taught Beth, who loved her poems, meter. Although Beth's area of study was English, she wasn't familiar with the intricacies of formal poetry, and was eager to learn about rhyme and meter. Catherine always said to me that Beth was the first and best reader of her poems. Beth was always a part of Catherine's dedications in the manuscripts she put together for publication.

UM: When did Catherine go to the Iowa Writers' Workshop? How did that come about?

MP: She went to Iowa at the behest of Donald Justice, and although she attended the writers' workshop she took an MA in 18th-century literature, although her MA thesis was a collection of poems. She had a hell of time in Iowa—in fact

June 21, 1996

Dear Don,

here is the manuscript at last. This was the
day I had hoped to mail it. But yesterday when I woke
up, the first thing I thought was that I had to get rid
of all those subtitles that indicate the seven parts
of the ms. Regretfully, I must say--but I finally realized
that it made the whole thing look gussied up. It hadn't
even occurred to me before. I think it was a hangover of
the years when I would think of the various titles for
my books at various times. So I have whited them out.
Unfortunately, there is too much white-out already. I would
have used new pages throughout with just the numbers
of the parts, but I am running out of bond paper. I did use
bond for the table of contents (I couldn't bear to type
those two pages over again). Too many pages have yellowed.

I struggled a long time with the arrangement of
the ms. I wanted some real continuity overall in spite
of the diversity, but I'm still afraid that it will merely
seem to go in all directions. I decided some time ago
that I wanted to return at the end to formal poems.

About the sonnets: I don't know when I hit on the
idea of the form, but that was what mostly engaged me.
The structure is the disjunctive syllogism (if, but, so)
--however, sometimes, in the second quatrain, the premise,
instead of being opposites, they are merely contrasts or
even intensives--and the tetrameters, especially with
all those feminine endings, I hoped would give it a lyrical
quality: logic with song. I also I liked the idea of end-
ing the sonnets with a trim trimeter. The ten sonnets I
chose for the ms. got a working over. There are still some
in notebooks.

I am grateful that you are willing to safeguard
the ms. Now we have the same three copies: mine and yours
and one for sending out to publishers.

This is a real relief to me. Thanks again.

Always the best to both,

Catherine

A letter from Catherine Davis to Donald Justice.

she raised hell in Iowa City, befriended many poets, writers, and artists and changed her approach to writing there; it's clear that her style changes. Not that she couldn't still rhyme and meter her way through a poem like nobody's business, but she also chose to write free verse.

UM: Did she ever share with you recollections of Iowa City? Anecdotes? How important was this time for her development as a writer?

MP: It was essential to her. As I said, it changed her style of poetry, perhaps because she was with younger poets in a kind of immersion situation.

UM: You say "she raised hell" in Iowa City and also mention her being a bit wild as a child. What do you mean? How did this wildness develop? Is there one specific story or instance that would reveal this side of her personality a bit?

MP: There are many specific stories.

UM: Did she talk at all about her community in Iowa? What did Catherine do after leaving Iowa City?

MP: Of those who were at Iowa, these are the names I remember: Michael Van Walleghen, Donald Justice of course, Harold Eastman and Gerald Manshiem, Dori Katz, Roger Rath and his wife Anne, Kathe Davis, Joe DeRoche, Martha Collins—anyway there are more names and she loved them all. She was quick to love.

She got her degree from the University of Iowa in 1964, then taught at California State Polytechnic College from 1966-1968, and the following two years taught at Northeast Missouri State College (now Truman State University) in Kirksville, Missouri. She placed herself in Still-Hildreth Osteopathic Hospital, which at one time had been a sanatorium for tuberculosis, but was then a place for recovering alcoholics as well as a mental institution. She started the poem "Still-Hildreth" there and was still re-working it when I first met her. An interesting side note is that Osteopathy was founded in Kirksville in a little cabin that's still there by Andrew Still—hence the name. MD's must have been rare in Kirksville.

UM: Can you tell us more about Catherine's experience at Still-Hildreth?

MP: Well the poem really talks about the place; she had funny stories about the AA meetings that were required. She was one of the few women—or maybe the only woman—attending, and the men would often talk of the fun they had when they were drunk, but were very obedient to the rules of the game during the meetings. There was a shrink there who found it odd and abnormal that Catherine had mainly younger friends. She really had a rest at Still-Hildreth. She found the grounds—it was former estate—a pleasure to walk around. It was a sanctuary for her.

UM: What did Catherine do after leaving Still-Hildreth?

MP: She moved to Boston in 1968. Before I met her, she had once again landed on hard times, and was living in rooming houses and working for awhile in a movie theater in what was then called the Combat Zone, an area on Washington Street in downtown Boston. It was notorious for X-rated theaters, strip joints, prostitutes, porn shops and most likely a drug trade. She wrote a poem about it, called "The Combat Zone or the Poetry of Fact." The Combat Zone is now gone.

She also sold her blood, which was type O-negative—rare and sought after because anyone can receive this blood type. Those with an O-negative blood type are universal donors but can only receive their own blood type. Her poem "Blood, Flesh, and Bones" is about this.

UM: You've given us a clear image of Catherine before you met. What was she like at the time you met her? And on that note, how did the two of you first meet?

MP: I met Catherine when she was hired at Thomas Todd Co., a printer on Beacon Hill. I had started to work there in 1969 and I think she was hired in 1970. Thomas Todd still had a composing room, proof presses for galleys, and compositors who prepared hand-set type and linotype for printing, whether letterpress or offset. Catherine was hired to be a second proof-reader. I worked as a clerk—wrote up orders, dealt with customers, and later on I also did estimates. It was a place that still had the feel of the 19th century. In fact the linotype and composing rooms operated on DC current.

She had a bead on me from the start, which perplexed me. She wooed me, which perplexed me even more, and in 1971 we moved in together. She was 20 years older than I and had lived such a different life from mine, and was a writer, a poet. I had never encountered a poet, nor had I ever encountered anyone like Catherine. She was a force majeure and I was intimidated by that strength. She packed a wallop and wasn't afraid to. My life was changed by Catherine, and for that I'm grateful.

UM: Can you think of a specific memory you have of your early life with Catherine that is in some way definitive? Something illustrative of your early relationship?

MP: I don't know how to answer this. We did a lot of stuff together. We didn't have much money —no one we knew did— but we managed to have fun. I was interested in photography, as was Catherine, and we spent hours at a photography gallery on Newbury Street, The Carl Sinbad Gallery, which showed contemporary photographers. Minor White was a big influence in the Boston area; he taught at MIT and had many acolytes who showed their work in Boston area galleries. The gallery also sold photography books and we spent hours there, treating the trove as a library. We also went to concerts and we spent a lot of time in Harvard Square and the Boston Public Library. Catherine had been a librarian and was a frequenter of libraries—I've since taken on that habit—as well as the MFA, the Gardner, bars, parties, friends' houses, etc. The usual life one has with someone.

But I didn't understand her fierce focus on poetry. I wasn't like Beth—I wasn't Catherine's first and best reader. This caused some friction between us, and later as she got more alienated from the idea of poetry—"poetry doesn't sell," "no one reads poems," "why write poetry"—she stopped writing altogether. When I first knew her Don Stanford had

just published her sonnets in *The Southern Review*, though she never wanted to be known as a "sonneteer." She was published subsequently, but as you know, she never succeeded in having a book published, not that she didn't try. I don't know if it was that her poems were out of fashion, or that she wasn't connected, or not in the right circles, or just bad luck—that for sure. Whatever it was, it wasn't fun.

We did have some fun together though. She instructed me; we read *The New Yorker*, enjoyed exploring science fiction, books on physics (obviously for the lay person), Stephen Jay Gould; politics was always on the plate, Watergate hearings a highlight, McGovern's defeat a low light. Bussing was a prominent issue in Boston in the late 60s and 70s and it was a fraught time and ugly. Catherine was obsessed by politics and there was a lot of politics to be obsessed about. The Vietnam War, Watergate, race issues, the radicalization of politics both black and white. The new Polish Pope, Solidarność, Lech Walesa, Havel, Romania, the breakup of the Soviet Union, Reagan. There was lots to talk about.

In turn, I taught her to like baseball, the Red Sox of course, and tennis, though much to my dismay she would always stand up for John McEnroe, no matter how impossible his behavior. But we both loved Stefan Edberg, an elegant player, who is now coaching Roger Federer.

UM: It seems that Catherine had a passion for so much beyond poetry and printing. We've also seen photographs of her elaborate mobiles, one of which is included in this book. Can you tell us something about how she came to make them?

MP: She got interested in mobiles—loved the artist Alexander Calder—and experimented with making them when she found the book *Mobile Design* by John Lynch, which instructed her in the techniques of mobile making. Once she discovered the book, off she went. Metals, veneers, jump rings, a workbench, a drill—she immersed herself as she always did. Catherine was never bland or tepid in anything that she did—it was full bore. I think it was the whimsy and the artifice of mobiles that intrigued her: they required a great deal of skill to create the illusion of simplicity and of course she loved their humor. Since money was scarce the materials were copper, tin, wire, but the woods were usually cherry and walnut veneers. She liked working with wood, and despite the fact that the cerebral palsy affected her left side she managed, as she did with printing, to work around the problem.

UM: At this time you were still living in Boston. Was Catherine teaching at all then?

MP: Through Martha Collins, Catherine got a teaching job at the University of Massachusetts-Boston, where she taught some women studies courses and taught Vietnam Vets. She liked teaching the vets—she liked teaching people who were eager to learn but then who wouldn't. Her last year of teaching she helped get a student get a partial fellowship at Stanford and was pleased at that accomplishment. She taught creative writing of course, as well as freshman composition, and I think she had some good times there before she left the University in 1988.

After that, she moved to Providence, Rhode Island, again poor—really poor this time—but Providence had a good public transportation system and a good library. We were still together then; I worked in Plymouth and went to Providence on weekends just like I had when she was in Boston. I had started at Plimoth Plantation in 1977—a living history museum that deals with the early Colonial history of Plymouth and the colony's relations with the Native Americans—so we lived apart during the week for years. We parted in 1993.

UM: What do you know of the last years of Catherine's life?

MP: Poverty takes a terrible toll on a person, and constant deprivation saps the spirit. The continuing straitened circumstances of her life eventually took their toll and also robbed her mind.

In 2000 I was contacted by the state of Rhode Island and the management company of the apartment complex where she lived because I was on record with the management company as her contact. They told me she was going to be evicted and told me when it would happen so I could be there. The Social Services people took her to a transitional facility to check on her health and to take care of her physical needs and then she was transferred to the nursing home and placed in the Alzheimer's unit.

I visited her in the nursing home, and was with her when she died in January of 2002. There's a funny story about what was on the bulletin board in her room—they must have asked her some questions about what she liked to do. And one of the points on the bulletin board about her interests was embroidery. It always made me laugh—although she she did darn socks when she was young, taught by her mother.

Stanford's
Creative Writing
Program

presents

Poems of
Catherine
Davis

a reading by
Kenneth Fields

April 30, 2008 at 7 pm
Margaret Jacks Hall
Building 460
Terrace Room, 4th floor

Refreshments served

Flyer for a reading in commemoration of the collection of
Catherine's work compiled by Helen Pinkerton Trimpi and
Suzanne J. Doyle. Designed by Marie Pelletier (2008) and
redesigned for inclusion in this book (2015).

PREFACE

Suzanne J. Doyle

Edgar Bowers introduced me to the work of Catherine Davis in 1973, while I was his student at the University of California, Santa Barbara. Sitting in his office, I mentioned that I liked Dorothy Parker's cynical epigrams. "The cynicism of a school girl," he scoffed. "You should read Catherine Davis."

Within the hour I had located *"for tender stalkes"* and one of her self-printed pamphlets, *The Leaves*, in the library, where I devoured and photocopied them. More than 30 years later, I still have those yellowed, dog-eared copies, dotted with marginalia—a crude map of the thematic and metrical obsessions of a lifetime. Partners and houses fell by the way, but I never lost Davis' poems, because I believe they poignantly give voice to what Janet Lewis called "the untranslatable heart."

The first section of a preface to an unnpublished manuscript of Catherine Davis's poems compiled and edited by Suzanne J. Doyle and Helen Pinkerton Trimpi in 2006.

When I returned to these poems after a long hiatus, I found the lines so familiar—their rhythms so deeply internalized—they echoed in my inner ear as though they were my own. But, these are far better lines than I have ever written: flawless iambics, perfect line breaks, coffin-nail closure, all in the unflinching hands of a moral sniper. The best of the epigrams rival the best of J. V. Cunningham, as this personal favorite illustrates:

> Cursed be the man whose higher seriousness
> Thinks no joke can survive, disdains finesse:
> May he meet all his life dry, witty bitches,
> Succumb to one at last, and die in stitches.

While the epigrams are outstanding, the lyrics are equally compelling, both in form and intensity. They are saturated with a sense of loss and failure. The voice—all too human, all too familiar—mourns that the heart cannot be schooled as strictly as stanzas. She is lazy and melancholy and wounded by those she loves. But, lucky for us, she follows her own good advice in *"for tender stalkes,"* so that we can be haunted and challenged by lines like:

> Make honey of your gall, my sorrow,
> And choice of this necessity;
> Prefer your indigence nor borrow
> From vacant love new destitution:
> Make unlike songs, secure but free.
> Let this be your full restitution.

I would burn every verse I've penned to write one such perfect stanza.

THE THEME OF LOSS IN THE EARLIER POEMS OF CATHERINE DAVIS

Helen Pinkerton Trimpi

Catherine Davis's best poems engage her readers on a profound level. Her "moral seriousness," to use F. R. Leavis's term for the quality of the great English and American novelists, is founded in an ethical sensibility that found its best expression in traditional stanza forms and in her faultless command of the traditional iambic line, whether long or short. In poems of rigorous self-scrutiny she explores such themes as temporal change ("The Leaves," "Patience"), acedia ("Nausea," "Indolence," "Obsession"), melancholy ("Idleness"), religious despair ("The Last Step"), the absence of—and hazards of—love (*"for tender stalkes"*), and other states of the contemporary soul in a language of moral analysis that she made her own. Nearly all of her early work is in traditional form.

This essay is a revision of "The Theme of Loss in the Earlier Poems of Catherine Davis and Edgar Bowers," *The Southern Review* Vol. IX, No. 3 (July, 1973), 595-616.

Her best poems are in the classical plain style of the Elizabethan and Jacobean poets—Wyatt, Ralegh, Donne, and Herrick—and are further influenced by the modern American plainness of Edwin Arlington Robinson, Louise Bogan and J. V. Cunningham. Her epigrams rival Cunningham's in their terse, satirical simplicity and power, although her subject matter is entirely her own: physical, emotional, and moral destitution. She read Catullus, Horace and Martial with passion and wrote about the literary world of New York as they did about Rome in poems such as "In New York," "They are not bees," "To a Little Editor," and "Beat."

Much of her best poetry deals with the theme of loss— that is, it concerns itself with evil in the older sense of privation of being and, hence, with experiences that range from the perception of death to the awareness of personal shortcomings. She deals with loss almost as a metaphysical absolute. In these poems she writes usually in a plain style, modeled eclectically upon the Latin epigrammatists and the earlier English poets mentioned above, although she does not invariably use this style, and her subjects—acute analysis of her own moral and emotional experience—are perfectly modern.

Three of her finest early poems, "Indolence," "The Leaves," and "Patience," reflect her inheritance of specifically American and nineteenth-century intellectual problems of the relation of the purely intellectual experience of the mind to the purely physical experience of the world of nature. In others she draws upon the general European inheritance, especially the satirical intentions and subject matter of the epigram. Fine examples arc "Insight 2: To the Spirit of Baudelaire," with its elegant verbal plays upon the "mantic bird" of demonic inspiration and the Holy Spirit of Christian tradition—the mantic bird being an inspiration to silence. Another is "Insight 5," with its muted apocalyptic vision:

> Pity, Catullus, these late revelers
> Who celebrate their passing with a shout,
> These idle, disabused malingerers
> Who wait defeat, as in a barbarous rout
> Amid a wreck of cities, empires lost:
> They are as faggots in a holocaust.
> Pity, among the rest, this sparrow verse.

There are six poems published roughly from 1957 to 1965 in which Davis comes most nearly to grips with her personal subject matter and writes what seem to me major poems. These are "Insight 8: Beware, old scrounger," "Insight 9: Comforting hope," "After a Time," "Under This Lintel," "The First Step," and "The Narrow House." All of these poems are about the experience of loss. Two of them, "The First Step" and "The Narrow House," deal with loss in terms that relate her experience to the Christian mystical tradition, in which willed loss—sacrifice—forms part of the discipline of self-abnegation—a "way" to God. The other four are related to what I call, for lack of a better term, the Romantic mystical tradition, where unwilled loss—suffering—is conceived as part of the poetic discipline, an essential way to the "nothingness" that is conceived as the ultimate human end. Davis uses the Christian scheme—loss as the way to being found—to define her difference from it; her strongest experience in the poems discussed belongs to the context of Romantic mystical thought.

Her epigrams "Beware, old scrounger" and "Comforting hope," together with the villanelle "After a Time," form a discussable group, each throwing light upon the others. The first two deal with the idea that death, though it is a part of the problem of loss, is also the solution to it. The experience behind both poems seems to be a confrontation with death, yet not the emotive near-experience of death which is the Christian "dying to the world" and which she touches upon in "The Narrow House." These poems are based on a recognition that one must eventually lose everything he has and everything he is, but the loss remains for the poet, consciously at least, an unwilled, involuntary loss. And it is an absolute loss. In contrast, the Christian would feel that it is by his own will that he accepts loss of all that he has and is, acquiescing thus in the will of God, without hope and without fear—even without love. "Beware, old scrounger" and "After a Time" make no reference to any Christian context as do "The First Step" and "The Narrow House," where Davis carefully distinguishes her experience from the Christian experience, in particular from that of St. Bernard. "Comforting hope" deals with recognition of the self as constantly afflicted by loss and as subsisting truly only in poverty.

Addressed to a habitual hard-luck case, "Beware, old scrounger" uses the figure of money to suggest the ultimate psychological state of such a person:

Beware, old scrounger, or, with winter come,
Your little impecuniosity
Will find at last the necessary sum
To cover all the waste there still must be:
All is the naked ground. And nothing, then,
Need fail you, who need never fail again.

The mood of the poem is the consciousness of imminent death, of the extreme condition in which a reversal could possibly take place. The scrounger does not recognize any indebtedness; he is not really thinking of paying back what he owes, but is rather obsessed with making his lack and his sense of it ever more complete. The poet recognizes this bent toward total waste and adapts the figure of money to it, ironically calling total loss "the necessary sum / To cover all the waste there still must be," drawing attention to the ultimately tragic nature of the "little impecuniosity" the scrounger is dallying with. The poem centers itself in the *sententia: "All is the naked ground."* The only "all" sufficient to satisfy the scrounger's indiscriminate craving for waste is the nothingness of death—the "naked ground." And the certainty of death includes the certainty of never lacking anything or of failing in any way, since there would be no existing being to sustain the lack or failure. The apparent simplicity and ease of diction and rhythm belie the ruthlessness of the statement. Davis has made use of a traditional European form and style in the epigram to embody an especially modern experience.

In "Comforting hope," she again uses the epigram magnificently, distinguishing two levels of suffering: that of physical cold, poverty, and discomfort, and that of self-contempt, bordering on despair:

> Comforting hope, how you have kept me warm!
> Not that I have not gone, in freezing storm,
> Head down against the wind, flat broke and sore,
> But that I did not see myself before
> As this mere fool, huddled, a shivering form
> In last year's ragged things, and nothing more.

The physical condition of poverty is overshadowed by the awareness of intellectual poverty: "last year's ragged things" are the old, outworn selves and attitudes one had hoped would last longer than their predecessors. Again, Davis brings, in one of her "insights," the exacting compression of the epigram and her complex modern perceptions into perfect realization.

The extraordinary villanelle "After a Time," perhaps her finest poem, deals with the experience of total loss, which is suggested as ultimate in "Beware, old scrounger." Again, the apparent simplicity and formality of the form and language are extreme:

> After a time, all losses are the same.
> One more thing lost is one thing less to lose;
> And we go stripped at last the way we came.
>
> Though we shall probe, time and again, our shame,
> Who lack the wit to keep or to refuse,
> After a time, all losses are the same.

No wit, no luck can beat a losing game;
Good fortune is a reassuring ruse:
And we go stripped at last the way we came.

Rage as we will for what we think to claim,
Nothing so much as this bare thought subdues:
After a time, all losses are the same.

The sense of treachery—the want, the blame—
Goes in the end, whether or not we choose,
And we go stripped at last the way we came.

So we, who would go raging, will go tame
When what we have we can no longer use:
After a time, all losses are the same;
And we go stripped at last the way we came.

The style, like the understanding which is the subject, is stripped and pure, leaving little for the critic to paraphrase. The poem recalls conventions of medieval lyric in its terse, aphoristic, and reiterative statement, but the content is non-Christian, a-religious determinism. The only poem like it that I know is J. V. Cunningham's epigram, "When I shall be without regret" (*The Poems of J. V. Cunningham,* ed. Timothy Steele, Swallow-Ohio UP, Athens, 1997, p. 41).

When I shall be without regret
And shall mortality forget,
When I shall die who lived for this,
I shall not miss the things I miss.
And you who notice where I lie
Ask not my name. It is not I.

Both poems confront the prospect of nothingness in the only intelligible manner possible, as the deprivation of positive being. The glamor of Wallace Stevens' "Snowman," who contemplates "nothing" in the beautiful symbol of snow, is absent in these poems, and both statements are for that reason truer and for me more moving. In these areas no one can touch Cunningham and Catherine Davis.

"Under This Lintel," a taunting address to pride, is marred somewhat by repetition and by difficult diction in the last stanza. It envisions at the moment of death the loss of pride, without any acquisition of humility (the "lintel stone" is death in William Dunbar's "Meditatioune in Wyntir," three lines of which form the epigraph):

> This is the stone, my pride;
> Under this you must bend,
> Under this you must break;
> Here I shall, though not mend,
> Not want you at my side,
> Do nothing for your sake.

Pride will be overcome in death because the poet herself will become "Only a mark"—a symbol without any being to signify:

> This is the stone: a place
> That is no place, my pride—
> Only a mark at last;
> Reach where you will, provide!
> This one pre-empted space
> Is mine, my one holdfast.

In the last stanza, by way of a negative verbal construction, Davis gets at the otherwise inconceivable condition of death in order to make the point that in death she will be so truly without pride that she will not even taunt pride any more—personified there as a shadow—with the fact of his defeat, as she taunts him now while alive:

> Under this lintel stone,
> Your limit, my support,
> I shall not, loath to cross,
> To fear no more this thwart
> Shadow, confront your own
> With this: THE MOST IS LOSS

The main feeling comes through almost as the result of a side effect: along with pride the poet, too, will be lost. She has condensed so much that the syntax is difficult to follow. The meaning, roughly, is that the way to defeat pride, whose demand is for "all," is to offer it "nothing." Pride's claim is absolute and can only be met by another absolute. This is a strange poem and more tortured in its thought and syntax than those discussed above, but it is still a fully realized and moving one. It seems to me that Davis has in these poems followed out to its intelligible limits the Romantic askesis of nothingness, using always a pure language of moral and philosophical understanding—almost without symbol and without glamorous figure. She has understood the lure; she has looked at the Medusa in the clear mirror of human rational conception and left little more to be said.

In "The Last Step" Davis grapples with the problem of pride again, this time by using a Christian context—the *scala humilitatis* of St. Bernard of Clairvaux—and declaring her difference from the experience of others in that context:

> The last step is the first.
> And so I have descended
> (Being of single mind)
> Through fifteen narrow years,
> And knew what I intended
> But not what I should find.

Her "last step" is the twelfth and bottom step in the scale of descent through pride that the lapsed, impenitent monk takes (or the virtuous monk contemplates in his self-scrutiny), as described in St. Bernard's *De gradibus humilitatem*. The scale descends from the top step, idle curiosity, down to the twelfth step, habitual sin. Davis's "first step"—the nature of which she probes throughout the poem—is the first and bottom step in the Benedictine scale of ascent in humility to which St. Bernard's descending scale corresponds. The Benedictine scale ascends from the first step, where one is ever mindful of God's commandments, to the twelfth step, where one walks always in complete humility with head bent and eyes upon the ground. On her "last step," Davis looks back "in dread" and sees no possibility of any ascent in humility, since only

> The downward flight, reversed,
> As I look back in dread,
> Ascends and disappears
> In shadow overhead.

In the second stanza, if it be correct to read "the laurel rood" as a figure for a combined poetic and religious self-discipline, perhaps such as Dante envisaged, she indicates how she differs from the tradition:

> What will the next step be?
> It should have been the climb,
> The ardent foot and hand
> Seeking the laurel rood.
> But I have come in time
> To know that where I stand
> Is not the place where he,
> Bernard, or some lost guide
> Who led me here, had stood
> Stripped of his lusts and pride.

She gives up "This figure of the stair" because

> The self unsatisfied
> Is what I find, Bernard,
> Not God; nothing but pride.

Being unable to take even the first step in the scale of humility—to fear God and obey his commandments—despite her experience of evil and retrospective reflection upon it, she asks:

> How does it help, sweet saint,
> To know our wretchedness,
> When there's no going back?
> How does it help to know
> By heart how comfortless

We are, how much we lack,
And what we fear? The taint
Of death, of broken meat,
I've tasted, too, and oh
How cold the food I eat!

Reiterating the plea for some meaning to be derived from
the knowledge of one's evil, she concludes that this self-
knowledge is hardly the cure for the condition:

I see both whence I came
And where I am, how far
I've drifted who preferred
My own fool vagrancy:
If, knowing this, I go
My own way all the same,
How does it help to know?

Anguish and helplessness are the subject of the poem,
not Bernardine or Benedictine discipline, but the good
which is the object of the discipline remains the implied
source of the feeling of loss. Like Baudelaire, Davis uses
historical Christian experience as a means of defining her
own difference from it. "The downward flight, reversed" for
her cannot really be taken; it can only be looked at. And the
looking at it is a form of self-punishing grief and remorse,
not at all the purgative scrutiny of sin in the light of faith
and love that St. Bernard defines as correlative with the
development of Benedictine humility. Where the poet is,
from St. Bernard's point of view, is on the last step taken
by the impenitent, excommunicate monk of whom Bernard

wrote, "When he can no longer either endure the living [the saved] or be endured by them, but must be carried out, I will continue faithfully to groan but will no longer pray with equal confidence" (trans. G. B. Burch). He is the lost one, and to him indeed the "downward flight, reversed, ... / Ascends and disappears / In shadow overhead." He does not, like Dante after having explored the various degrees of Hell by descending through them, find his movement reversed as he begins to ascend from the center of the earth and to climb the Purgatorial mountain.

The last three stanzas with the repeated phrase "How does it help?" achieve their power as lament from the precision with which the Christian context has been invoked, dealt with, and set aside as irrelevant. The poet understands her condition and has found in tradition the figurative and moral terms to define it. Of course, the figure of the "impenitent monk" that is implicit in "the last step" may, by extension, represent any human betrayal or loss of a cherished good. Loss is defined here in a tradition of careful definition of moral conditions which gives to her language great precision and resonance. "The First Step" is a lament of great power. Elsewhere Davis defines the lost person movingly in terms of the damned, for example in "Making an End," where she echoes Dante's imagery:

There comes a moment when the vision clears,
And we must start to learn
To bide the fire of ice and snow,
To live with that abyss
Of cold to come, to know the heart
Of horror to the heart,
Or else, as birds of passage, turn and turn.

The subject of "The Narrow House," which is subtitled *"In angusta domo,"* is the condition of the "twice-dead," the dead who are damned and hence "dead" in both body and soul. The poem deals with the attempt and the failure to comprehend imaginatively their condition and with the need to pity them. The form is that of the song written in stanzas with a refrain, conventional in the Scottish Chaucerians and Wyatt. This poem comes closer to St. Bernard's "way" of self-scrutiny and purgation than the poem that alludes to him, as Davis tries to comprehend the "narrow house"—the absolutely lost state of the dead who are damned—which is the truth of the final human condition without grace, as St. Bernard envisioned it. Moreover, it seems to be an attempt to confront the "abyss of loss," which is the essence of the Christian mystical endeavor. As a statement about this the poem is invaluable, though the attempt is a self-confessed failure. In terms of each of four of the senses—hearing, smell, touch, and sight ("averted")—she considers the state of "those cast out, who had no place / But the narrow house." The mind, then, appalled by its vision, sought

> . . . the ground of love and rest
> And willingly was dispossessed
> Of the narrow house,

It may be noted that in turning away from the narrow house, even to seek God—the "ground of love and rest"—the mind would make its mistake from the Christian point of view. The poet, quite justly and as scrupulously as the Christian, criticizes this dispossession as simply action taken out of fear:

So love was the recurring dread
Of the abyss of loss instead,
From which same fear the heart had fled
    From the narrow house.

The Christian, theoretically, would not refuse the abyss
of loss out of fear or anything else, but would embrace it
willingly, trusting in God, and not actively seeking him,
but waiting for God to seek him. Then, the poet's mind and
heart, having fled in fear from the abyss of loss, finds no
rest, for,

Unrest turned a bare, fugitive
Existence, which at most could give
Change from the change in which they live
    In the narrow house.

Who sees them once as not unique
But kindred creatures still must seek
Lost gentleness, gently to speak
    For the narrow house.

In this poem Davis again, though less directly, defines her
relation to the Christian mystical tradition, using it to state her
inability to achieve the experience it deals with and to define
movingly her own. But, like Wallace Stevens' putting aside of
Christianity in "Sunday Morning," only in appearance is what
is put aside here the Christian love of God, for that love is not
altogether accurately seen. As I indicated above, Christian
mystical love is not fear, not "the recurring dread / Of the
abyss of loss" but, beyond fear and hope, it is acceptance of

the abyss of loss if that should happen to be God's will. She is correct in Christian terms to criticize anyone's turning to the "ground of love and rest," if what turns him to the "ground" is fear of the "abyss." Davis does, however, state her acceptance of total loss in "After a Time" without relating it at all to the Christian point of view. The context of "After a Time," possibly her best poem, is non-Christian, modern, and secular, as already noted.

A LEARNED DISTRUST

Kenneth Fields

By little chances I have learned distrust
Even you, Tycho, god of small things, are dust.
                                        —C.D.

Nearly fifty years ago my sweetest and most innocent colleague, Lucio Ruotolo, paused with his briefcase in the cloakroom of the Stanford Faculty Club, and asked Virgil Whitaker, our Chairman for Life, "Do you think this is safe here?" And Virgil answered like a good Renaissance scholar, "Nothing is safe in this world of sin and woe"—a Stoic reply that would have amused Catherine Davis because it underlies the psychology of most of her work.

Stoicism, rather than versions of Platonism or Buddhism, ought to be the perennial philosophy because it is suited to hard times, which is to say, any time. And Davis had more than her share even before she got to Stanford.

To simplify, Seneca, the Roman Stoic in word if not in practice, believed we ought to cultivate fortitude to endure the caducities of life, preparing ourselves for loss. In the 91st epistle, he writes of the despondency of his friend Liberalis, whose hometown Lyons, the capital of Gallic Rome, has just been utterly destroyed by fire. The unexpectedness of this holocaust causes Seneca to assert that we should be at all times inured against disaster: "This is a reason for ensuring that nothing ever takes us by surprise. We should project our thoughts ahead of us at every turn and have in mind every possible eventuality instead of only the usual course of events."

Davis had a rough life, never far from poverty. Her father went to prison for armed robbery when she and her sister were babies, and she never saw him again. She and her sister were raised by a mother we'd call abusive today. Her poem "She" is about her mother ("hell on wheels"), whom she ironically praises for giving her her toughness ("she gave as good as she got and here I am"). She had a slight case of cerebral palsy, misdiagnosed as polio, which affected one side of her body. When her mother discovered that Davis was a lesbian, she drove her to the train station and never saw her again. Nor, I think, did Davis ever see her sister. Catherine Davis was sixteen years old.

Her stoic determination stood her in good stead, along with her enormous talent and intelligence, getting her to the University of Minnesota to study with Robert Penn Warren, Chicago to study with J. V. Cunningham, and Stanford, on a Creative Writing Fellowship, to study with Yvor Winters, who loved her work and put seven of her epigrams in the anthology *Quest for Reality*. At the age of 37 she earned her AB from George Washington University, and then she entered the Iowa Writers' Workshop where she studied with Donald Justice.[1] She continued to publish poems and function as an itinerant teacher, taking other jobs as she could, before her alcoholism, mental illness, and Alzheimer's disease took their toll, sometimes leaving her indigent, surviving, as Marie Pelletier has said, on Kit Kat bars and beer. She knew about loss.

Her best-known poem, a villanelle beginning "After a time all losses are the same," was published in the influential anthology *New Poets of England and America* (1957), edited by Donald Hall, Robert Pack, and Louis Simpson. It may be bookended by two more famous villanelles, Dylan Thomas's "Do Not Go Gentle," a poem that Davis seems to be replying to, and Elizabeth Bishop's "One Art," a poem surely instigated by Davis's poem. When I mentioned this to Donald Hall many years ago, he said he hadn't thought of it, but was going to teach the two poems that way from then on. J. V. Cunningham especially liked the opening lines:

> After a time, all losses are the same.
> One more thing lost is one thing less to lose;
> And we go stripped at last the way we came.

For Thomas's "Rage, rage against the dying of the light" Davis concludes

> So we, who would go raging, will go tame
> When what we have we can no longer use:
> After a time, all losses are the same;
> And we go stripped at last the way we came.

When set beside "After a Time," "One Art" seems breezy and, to me, far less powerful. Davis's poem and all the others in this volume need to be remembered. We used to say, "publish or perish," as if the choices were mutually exclusive.

Davis herself understood how fragile the survival of her poems might be, and she expresses this in her references to the Roman poet Catullus. In "Passerculi" (little sparrows) she at once refers to Catullus as well as the rhetorical formula of the lesser contrasted to the greater—Sappho staking her territory of amorous passion against Homeric epic warfare is one example. Davis is thinking of Catullus mourning the death of Lesbia's sparrow, one of the little things (like all of us) destined to be lost in the obliterating underworld.

> If you would have dark themes and high-flown words,
> Great albatrosses drenched in sacredness,
> Go read some other book; for I confess
> I cannot make my verses to your taste,
> And though they are not trifles made in haste,
> Mine are to those such light things, little birds,
> Sparrows among their kind, whose one last shift
> Is shelter from the universal drift.

The satire aimed at the current literary crowd is more pointed in "In New York," which she calls Second Rome, but with a difference: "These toadies like the toads they toady to." More biting and perhaps more problematic, this poem, set, I think, in New York on New Year's Eve:

Pity, Catullus, these late revelers,
Who celebrate their passing with a shout,
These idle, disabused malingerers
Who wait defeat, as in a barbarous rout
Amid a wreck of cities, nations lost:
They are as faggots in a holocaust.
Pity, among the rest, this sparrow verse.

It's odd formally, seven lines, with the final rhyme oblique and distant (five and seven steps away), and yet with definitive closure. It's the sixth line that catches our eye now, and it concludes the only couplet in the poem. But I think it strikes for other reasons too. We know what this line denotes, but the violent and horrific connotation, surely intended, nearly overturns the poem. But what's most peculiar is the quiet afterthought that includes the poet and her work as well: "Pity, among the rest, this sparrow verse." Sparrows were associated with lechery—they pull Aphrodite's chariot in Sappho's great ode. The satirist associating herself with the satirized is an unforgettable moment in epigrammatic poetry.

As the poems go on, one can see some relaxation, a sense of accepting, letting in, rather than pushing away, as she seems to understand what her stoicism has cost her. It's possible to be so obsessed with loss, that you run from what you have in the vain attempt to control loss; to quit before you are fired. From "Obsession": "Dreading what still must be, I run / Lost to what is for what is not." And from "I Need More Light":

I hurt who hurts me not to be alone,
And then, alone, I hate the hurt I give;
I need more light, or to be made of stone.

In the beautiful sequence on love, *"for tender stalkes,"*
she writes:

Now the heart stops and stops forever.
We cannot keep the things we keep.
And so, willful, we quickly sever
Ourselves from what we love, toward sleep.

And again:

But then I think how restless I
Have been with love, how I would toss
And turn, would, though with love, still lie
Alone, possessed by an unknown loss.

What we may see as these poems change is critical self-reflection, as if she's looking at her character itself, through shifts in style, the work of mastery of a very high order. In poems not included in this selection, which I hope will be available soon, along with notebooks, in an archive, we watch her, even while working selling tickets in a rundown theater in Boston's Combat Zone—where the down and out come for sex and other kinds of relief from heat and cold. We see Davis as a woman noticing her surroundings with compassion, knowing what it's like to need a drink as much as they do. If Davis had been a street photographer, we'd know how to value these shots. It's pointless to wonder what she might have been like as a writer in less straitened circumstances, but I wonder anyway. Richard Savage had nothing on her; Doctor Johnson would have loved Catherine Davis.

I want to conclude with "A Small River in Iowa and the Wide World." It is an island of calm in a terrible life that was to get worse—a deeply moving poem in the midst of work characterized by my friend Bradin Cormack as "the sad reaches of a wounded psyche." The convention is romantic, and she's at home in her pastoral setting, looking at "only water." As in so many modern poems that M. H. Abrams has shown us, she is in colloquy with someone who is now absent—and the poem is beautifully free of rancor:

> We talked that other hour of love, but not
> Of mine, of yours for someone else. Now all
> This afternoon I've thought of love and you,
> Who are not here. The wide world makes a knot
> Of spirit bones flesh blood dark love loss gall.
> And yet the grass, come night, is laced with dew.

There's no need to point out the great line—everyone can hear its distinctive cadence, its equal found only in Emerson. She knows she will soon leave Iowa and this scene, and she wonders if she'll bring it back to mind later.

> When all these that were shimmer, shadow, or gloss
> Are far from here, shall I remember then
> The river as a world wide as wonder
> That flows, entwines continuous change with loss?
> Having once been, shall I be once again
> Aware of earth's both excellence and plunder?

We can only hope so. A magnificent masterpiece, it stands in relation to her earlier poems, to her native idiom, as Louise Bogan's late poem "Night" stands to hers:

—O remember
In your narrowing dark hours
That more things move
Than blood in the heart.

Stanford, California
January 31, 2015

NOTE

[1] For some of these facts and others I am grateful to Helen Pinkerton Trimpi, who knew Catherine Davis, and to Suzanne Doyle, whose remark "moral sniper" stays in the mind. Without their efforts, along with the cooperation of Marie Pelletier, Davis's partner of many years, it is doubtful that these poems would be seeing the light of day.

A DANCING STEP: THE POEMS OF CATHERINE DAVIS

Michael Van Walleghen

The poems of Catherine Davis reveal, with elegant precision, a poetic self as brave and dauntless as any murdered, persecuted, or otherwise exiled Russian poet of the 20th century. These poems are almost entirely about loss—a lot of pain and hard reckoning here—but overall they demonstrate a stubborn refusal to give in, or give up the pursuit of a poetic excellence her often dire circumstance would seem to disallow. These are poems that Sir Thomas Wyatt, Herrick, or John Donne would almost certainly recognize and admire, I think, for their wit, clarity and formal beauty—considerations that would seem to be increasingly rare in the poetry we find these days in even the best of our current magazines and journals.

Although these poems seem to come flying straight out at us from that dismal and familiar "dark night of the soul" that drove so many 20th century American poets to alcohol and madness (Catherine Davis, too, it's necessary to say), there is an entirely admirable heroism to be found here, a striving toward the light, a steady refusal to give up or give in, or let her work swerve into mere self pity. Instead, she follows, as best she can, the Socratic path to self-knowledge, even if it should avail nothing in the end but more pain—as in the following stanza from her poem "What Does It Mean? " after Thomas Wyatt:

> I toss, I turn, I cough, I curse;
> I must, it seems, all night rehearse,
> Revile my days and make them worse.
>   What does it mean?

The Thomas Wyatt poem "Of the Pains and Sorrows Caused by Love," from which the refrain "What does it Mean" is taken, seems entirely more conventional by comparison—a routine sixteenth-century complaint, a meditation on the Pains and Sorrows of courtly love, an almost formulaic topic of the time. For Catherine Davis, on the other hand, the Pains and Sorrows of her own experience are a matter of life and death. There is no answer other than that.

But what l am most aware of, above all else, in these poems is the joy and exuberance of her art, the little victories of closure, rhyme and meter her tight formal constraints seem to encourage—plus the unexpected and continual surprise of her insights, and the crisp liveliness of her diction. Despite Catherine's grinding poverty, alcoholism and incipient madness, these poems provide a bedrock of order, a brief respite from all the demons of her existential chaos.

These poems move so gracefully, and with such assurance, they seem to me to almost dance to their conclusions. And I can't help but be reminded here of a little phrase by the great Polish poet Zbigniew Herbert, who ends his poem "Request" by wishing, from his patron god Hermes, a final gift of a "dancing step." I have a picture of Catherine from our Iowa City days stuck in my mind, however, limping through the snow in below zero weather with neither hat nor gloves and absolutely a million light years from anything like a dancing step. And while the agony and desperation of her everyday life abide in my memory, it is her genius as a poet to be able to transform it finally into an unlikely and dazzling art that will surely outlive us all. Catherine expresses her own inkling of this redemptive promise in a wonderful adversion to the wisdom of Catullus in section three of her poem *"for tender stalkes,"* a fitting way, I think, to remember this consummate artist at her most committed, essential best.

> The bitter waste, the long distraction,
> The graveclod heaviness within,
> Passion, become a numbed inaction,
> Ravage both love and discipline.
>
> Catullus brought to passion skill,
> To anger wit, and eased and mended
> His bruised heart and his baffled will
> In waking song, when love was ended.
>
> Make honey of your gall, my sorrow,
> And choice of this necessity;

Prefer your indigence nor borrow
From vacant love new destitution:
Make unlike songs, secure but free.
Let this be your full restitution.

December 7, 2015

CATHERINE DAVIS: STYLES, THEMES, FORMS

William Edinger

Catherine Davis's deepest and most enduring stylistic commitment is to a traditional form of the plain style. The poets whom Davis mentions, imitates, or echoes—Catullus, William Dunbar, Sir Thomas Wyatt, J. V. Cunningham—suggest its models. The commitment is a risky one inasmuch as the traditional plain style offers little in the way of the obviously poetic. Because it cultivates directness, conciseness, and clarity, typically prefers bare statement to description, and employs the unselfconscious language of reflection, plain-style poetry may strike readers accustomed to more eloquent, imagistic, or mannered styles as unimaginative and prosaic. We know that only after the twentieth century's unprecedented diversification of styles and tastes greatly enlarged the possibilities of poetic reception did Wyatt's plain-style songs and verse epistles, long neglected in favor of his work in the ornate genre of the Petrarchan sonnet, become fully capable of affording what an Aristotelian critic would call their "proper pleasures."[1]

What are these? In Davis as in Wyatt and Cunningham especially, the discursive pleasures (if we may distinguish these for the moment from pleasures more strictly and immediately formal) are primarily intellectual and ethopoeic. Davis resembles Wyatt and Cunningham in writing as a clear-sighted conscientious analyst and judge of her emotional and moral experience and also as a satirist no less clear-sighted and judgmental about the failings of others. In introspective poems such as Wyatt's "It was my choice, it was no chance," Cunningham's "Convalescence" and "Distraction," and Davis's "Discretion," "Routine," and "Under This Lintel," the plain-style poet seems to write in colloquy with another or herself, and the reader eavesdrops. But of course poets write to and for imagined audiences, imagined kinds of readers. At the beginning of his book of Epigrammes, the plain-style master Ben Jonson defines his readership by advising:

> Pray thee, take care, that tak'st my book in hand,
> To read it well: that is, to understand.

Much of Davis's best work affords the satisfaction of following a clear, economical and eminently reasonable process of reflection through to a completed act of understanding. This act may be provisional; it may acknowledge uncertainty or complexities beyond its reach; but within its limits it affords something gratifyingly intelligible and ponderable. The plain style itself is reasonable in privileging the communicative virtues of written language. Clarity and simplicity invite sympathetic understanding by capturing the recognizable and shareable, by identifying what is implicitly general in private experience. Conciseness, avoiding the clutter of the merely idiosyncratic and the transiently circumstantial, enhances sharcability—and perhaps also the process of discovery itself—by keeping the poet focused on significance. Such writing gains an ethopoeic force beyond its merely intellectual value by embodying the moral virtues of dignity and integrity—virtues that can humanize the barest language and engage our sympathies accordingly. The plain style at its best makes good on Whitehead's dictum that style is the ultimate morality of mind.

Dignity is grounded in respect for others and for oneself. Davis's style respects its readers by being unmanipulative, by aiming at transparency rather than at making an impression. (See "Before You Enter," a poem that among other things is an allegory of reading.) Her style conveys the dignity of self-respect through its reticence about autobiographical particulars: it observes a decorum of privacy. However attractive in writing, reticence and privacy as lived may be problematic, especially in intimate relationships; this is Davis's subject in "Insight" # 4, "Discretion," "A Few Quiet Days," and "Finding Ourselves and Others." Robust self-respect—dignity as active integrity—informs her satirical vision, notably in epigrams #s 2, 6, and 11 of "Insights." These are poems that share Wyatt's principled contempt for the hypocrisy, opportunism, and game-playing that he endured at court and Davis found in certain literary circles.

Dignity and integrity safeguard a core self. This, for Davis, must be a reasonable self, ideally capable of understanding, choosing, willing, carrying through. But her poems of self-examination often show reason under assault from forces both external and internal. Reason and the core self are eroded by the dullness, distraction, and fatigue of "Routine," challenged by the behavior of intimately-known others ("Insight # 4," "I Need More Light"), threatened more insidiously and gravely by unmanageable passion and "The random terrors of the heart" ("What Does It Mean? after Thomas Wyatt") and by neurotic behaviors and reactions experienced as alien to the self ("Obsession," "Nausea," "Belongings," "The Unprofitable Servant," *"for tender stalkes"*).

Poems of still deeper consideration find reason itself to be problematic. Wyatt knew, as a matter of unchallenged cultural inheritance, that his reason was a gift of God. For Davis, reason enjoys no such objective warranty; its justification can only be existential. For her, the skies are "god-deserted" ("Arachne: An Ode"), and heaven is no longer "the haven-portal, / To restless flesh the ground of rest / And love . . ." (*"for tender stalkes,"* # 5).[2] Life ends permanently with death. In a powerful poem, "The First Step," Davis clarifies the predicament of the modern believer in reason by invoking certain lost strengths of Christian moral experience. The poem alludes to St. Bernard's twelve-step ladder of humility and pride, down which one descends through degrees of selfishness to habitual sinfulness and alienation from God, and up which one ascends towards forgiveness, selflessness, and spiritual renewal. The poet, imagining herself at the bottom of the ladder, recognizes that, for her, ascent is no longer a possibility. She understands that dignity and integrity have forfeited their alliance with the Christian humility necessary to the upward climb because humility presupposes submission to a divine authority and providential order which for her do not exist. She recognizes that the natural modern ally and support of dignity and integrity is pride, love's great antagonist and the source of her isolation (see "Under This Lintel" and "The Narrow House"). And she recognizes as well that her reason cannot save her because it has no activating power: incapable of praxis, it functions merely as passive understanding. So the question she puts to it is: "How does it help to know?"[3]

———— ◆ ————

"Better that we see clearly, truly," the poet judges in a later poem ("*for tender stalkes*"); understanding is preferable to its alternatives even if reason acts only as spectator and interpreter. This is its role in a number of poems that move beyond the plain style's traditional limitations by making use of natural description. That Davis possessed the seeing eye is apparent from her one unabashedly virtuosic exercise in observation and description, the dazzling "The Willows in Winter in the Boston Public Garden." Her usual descriptive procedures subordinate natural description more completely to thematic purposes.

These link Davis to the great Romantic and post-Romantic tradition of poetic inquiry into our responsiveness to the world's physical beauty. Davis makes use of several of the possibilities uncovered by this tradition. In "Indolence" she invokes the Wordsworthian faith in the language of nature only to reject it. She wanders in a grove "Where all sound was indefinite" and realizes that whatever congruence she senses between the indolence of August days and her own indolence is more a matter of mood than meaning; her future will issue from human "half-intentions" unrelated to "the underspeech of leaves." Yet at the same time she projects a future governed more by natural (unwilled, unconscious) processes than by reasonable agency, a future imagined as lifting and subsiding like "a casual, shaken bough." The implications of these natural / human contrasts and comparisons become clearer in the next poem, "The Leaves." The leaves themselves, the poem declares, are merely part of the fixed seasonal processes of growth and decay that characterize the general unconsciousness of nature, and so know nothing of their enforced cyclical destiny and imminent "destitution." But we, as conscious, imaginative, reflective beings, cannot help finding "Some likeness for the mind" in such phenomena. The difficulty for Davis is this. Whereas a Wordsworthian optimist would interpret the impulse to humanize nature as a sign that the natural world belongs as much to us as we to it, and that this impulse helps make us feel at home in it as well as making us more fully human, Davis suspects that our imaginative likeness-finding is merely a trick of the mind, and our humanizing of nature a reassuring delusion. She suspects that nature's real lesson, as a matter of cold fact, is that we belong only too fully to its processes and enjoy nothing like the freedom of choice and will on which we pride ourselves.

Davis doubtless expects her leaves to bring to mind the insentient and unpersonified leaves of Louise Bogan's "Simple Autumnal" as well as the personified, helplessly passive leaves of Shelley's "Ode to the West Wind" (see stanza four of "I Need More Light"). Davis's "The Leaves" suggests in conclusion that "we were but the mark / Of change, not more secure" against unconscious and irresistible natural forces than the leaves and blackbirds of "Patience," nor more finally significant than the lintel in "Under This Lintel," which is "Only a mark at last." This may recall Stevens' "Death is absolute and without memorial / As in a season of autumn ...." In "Belongings," another poem of leaves and birds, Davis alludes to Stevens' "The Course of a Particular" and its "cry of leaves that do not transcend themselves"; but in her poem she hears no cry and, avoiding personification, sees in the physical world's "usual drift / Of all expendables ... What she belonged to, what belonged to her." She returns to a traditional kind of personification in "The Summer Leaves," treating the leaves at summer's end as emblems of human change and loss.

————◆————

I have emphasized discursive qualities of style. Since discursive effects are finally inseparable from the verse-forms that present them, the verse-forms too deserve some notice. Like most English and American poets of her generation, Davis began as a so-called formalist, writing in traditional accentual-syllabic meters (iambic trimeter, tetrameter, pentameter), rarely in pentameter blank verse ("Belongings," "An Ordinary Sunday Morning in Iowa City"), and in a variety of stanzas and rhyme-schemes, regular and irregular, including the notably formal terza rima ("I Need More Light") and villanelle ("After A Time"). Later in her career she took up less traditional forms—syllabic meters ("The Passing of Eden," "Finding Ourselves and Others") and different modes of free verse ("Teacher," "Railroads," "To an Archaeologist . . .")—and she devised nonce forms, whether strict ("The

[163]

Summer Leaves") or more irregular ("Before You Enter," "Finding a Way," "The Willows in Winter . . ."), which are hard to label.

Through most of these poems and forms Davis's diction remains plain and, apart from its purity, unremarkable; yet the quality of feeling communicated varies widely from poem to poem depending on its verse-form. Fixed form and obvious patterning in accentual-syllabic verse often produce an impersonal and elevated effect quite independently of diction—as witness the plain language but ceremonial majesty of the villanelle "After a Time." Because their insistent musicality emphasizes the poem's status as a special artistic discourse, the traditional accentual-syllabic meters, especially trimeter and tetrameter, tend to distance and elevate, to make impersonal, and to impart a kind of rhythmical authority. These qualities lend distinction to the distilled, essentialized simplicity which so much of Davis's work shares with that of Wyatt and Cunningham. On the other hand, syllabic meters, and some forms of free verse and accentual meter, by relaxing into the irregularity of speech rhythms, allow plain language to seem comparatively more spontaneous and intimate, more expressive of individuality or personality, and the reader to feel more immediately present or more directly addressed (see "The Passing of Eden," "Teacher," "Before You Enter"). These forms may also suit attempts to articulate penumbral kinds of awareness whose tentativeness or subtlety might elude the more energetic and decisive movement of accentual-syllabic verse. A case in point is the remarkable "Finding a Way," a poem that hints at its formal capabilities while enacting them.

Through all this considerable variety of forms and effects Davis remains at heart a formalist. We see this in her liking for fixed stanzas and for rhyme even in syllabics ("Finding Ourselves and Others," "Before You Enter") and free verse and nonce forms ("Finding a Way," "The Willows in Winter . . .," "The Summer Leaves"). Stanza and rhyme are means of emphasizing (however subliminally) the poet's formal control over her material, and perhaps of helping the poet maintain that control. In Davis, the less traditional and the apparently more casual verse-forms both typically observe a parsimony linking them to the poems in accentual-syllabic meters. The virtues of clarity and conciseness characterize her work as a whole.

NOTES

[1] *Poetics*, 14.9-11; 23.16-20; cf. *Nicomachean Ethics*, 10.5.1-2, 6-7.

[2] "Arachne: An Ode" is not included in the present collection but is available at www.poetryfoundation.org. [editors' note]

[3] These remarks on Davis's "The First Step" are indebted to Helen Pinkerton Trimpi's essay, "The Theme of Loss in the Earlier Poems of Catherine Davis and Edgar Bowers," *The Southern Review*, Vol. IX, New Series (July 1973), 595-616.
A later version of this essay is included in the present volume, pp. 129-144. [editors' note]

ON CATHERINE DAVIS'S "A FEW QUIET DAYS"

Carol Moldaw

As someone who likes to write in undetected privacy, I felt an immediate connection to Catherine Davis's "A Few Quiet Days," an ars poetica that maps out the dialectics of the artistic process with deep understanding and wit. Written in the imperative, it reads as a set of instructions—to the self, to a reader—on how to "seem" and how to be, in order to create. What struck me first was the second stanza's directive for evading others:

> If busy eyes pursue,
> Practice an old deceit:
> Be sure they see in you
> Idleness and retreat.

That this deceit is posited as "old"—something long practiced, no doubt out of perceived necessity—and that "idleness and retreat" are the artist's protective covering, I find poignant as well as darkly humorous, a kind of inside joke, for what writer hasn't been accused of listless uncommunicative daydreaming? It seems at first that this is what the poem is about: how to achieve a "quietness" so that "none … suspects" what you are up to. The refuge from "busy eyes" buys the "you" time, time that "will have an end/But shall be yours no less." Time that is yours—who could ask for anything more?

In the third and fourth quatrains and the concluding one-line stanza, though, when the poem expands on "quietness," it goes beyond this depiction of hide-and-seek to achieve a resonant description of the creative process:

> And if you seem to sleep,
> Then be content to seem.
> Let stillness grow so deep
> That none, in this extreme
>
> Of instants motionless,
> Suspects the active part,
> The running wakefulness
> That stays the mind and heart:
>
> True mentor of your art.

While stillness is again posited as a protective covering, it is also, and more essentially, the conductive medium through which the "active part" of creativity, "the running wakefulness," can flow (undetected). One of the masterful strokes of this description is that only the word "part" suggests the interdependence of the "instants motionless" and "the running wakefulness." Wakefulness needs the quiet in order to stream; without the wakefulness, stillness runs the risk of turning into sleep. The complex interplay between these is encapsulated in the verb "stays," which suggests a halting of "the mind and heart" but is better understood as a securing or balancing of them.

Davis chose a balanced meter, a-b-a-b rhyming trimeter quatrains, to write about the conditions conducive to the creation of art. The first two stanzas are enclosed. The third and fourth, where the poem opens up, are grammatically connected, with the noun phrase "extreme of instants motionless" broken at "extreme" to end the stanza. As "extreme" hangs in the balance—extreme of what?—we feel the equipoise of the "instants motionless" and "active part" that are to come. That the poem then continues past the framework of quatrains to balance on the pivot of a last b-rhyming line, "true mentor of your art," shows Davis' consummate mastery. The word "mentor" gave me pause: at first reading I was tempted to twist its meaning a little and think of it as a synonym for "nurturer" or even "motor." In the end, though, what I find wonderful and startling is the suggestion that the counselor and guide to "your art" is the process at its center.

REMEMBERING CATHERINE: IOWA CITY

Kathe Davis

Catherine Davis widened my world.
I arrived in Iowa City in the summer of 1965, a naive country-grown 22-year-old there for just a summer in the Writers' Workshop. After a year away, I came back, as so many returned to Iowa City, and stayed almost another two years.

The 60s were a great time to be in Iowa City. A terrible time, too, I suppose, for some people: what was happening there would, in retrospect, define the iconic 60s, "free love," the sexual revolution generally, the domestication of marijuana, innocently dubbed "grass," and other less innocuous drugs, including and especially LSD, foremost among the hallucinogens. Those didn't all work out well for everyone. But for me Iowa City meant more freedom, knowledge of an expanding universe, literal & metaphorical— and Catherine Davis was part of that.

I wanted to think of myself as a poet, but the truth was that I was much more interested in living a life than writing about it, and lacked the discipline to spend the necessary time alone in a room trying to get it right. One of the many gifts Catherine gave me was a demonstration of what it meant to value poetry above nearly all else. She was a living example of genuine literary dedication. She caused me to take literature in general, and poetry in particular, more seriously.

Catherine was already a fixture in Iowa City when I got there, though I met Martha Collins first, because she was managing The Paper Place bookstore, and I gravitated, like any reading addict, to the bookstore before anywhere else. Also I needed a job, had bookstore (and library) experience, and was soon hired.

The Paper Place was the store where poets shopped and sometimes congregated in the narrow aisles between the high, dark, hand-built shelves innocent of security cameras or even mirrors. I met Catherine, probably there, early on. I heard about her before I met her. Someone must have told me that there was a poet in town named Catherine Davis, and at least two people asked if I was "*the* Catherine Davis." I wish I remembered what Catherine herself said about the similarity of our names when we met, but I do not—only that it was funny. She had a wonderful wry sense of humor.

I was in awe of the fact that Catherine had actually known Yvor Winters, had been his student. I had recently discovered his critical collection *In Defense of Reason*, which charmed me first of all by its title. Coming from an emotional and somewhat disordered family background, I over-valued "reason" and the emotional restraint Winters advocated. I loved Winters' magisterial tone and his utter certitude, even when he was clearly entirely wrong.

Catherine had learned or developed some of that same fixity of opinion and judgment, with a marvelous clarity about her reasons and an impressive ability to articulate them. My guess is that her attraction to mid-century formalism was a matter not merely of literary fashion or instruction, but that it served as compensation for or counter-actant to the "disorder and early sorrow" of her chaotic early family situation.

For two years at the University of Chicago (1948-1950), Catherine had studied with the poet, epigrammatist, and critic J V Cunningham (1911-1985). Cunningham, early associated with Winters, is little-known now—"America's Best Forgotten Poet," in the title phrase of Joseph Bottum's 1998 review of *The Poems of J. V. Cunningham*.[1] But in the mid-60s he was at the height of his powers and production, and the bookstore carried his work. Catherine put me onto that work, singing the praises of Cunningham and his skill. (She remained glowingly appreciative, almost adulatory, of the teachers who had meant the most to her and from whom she had learned the most. She was acutely aware always, I think, of how different a life from the one for which she seemed destined she had because of their instruction, friendship, and sometimes intercession. Her habit was to credit them rather than her own talent, intelligence, and hard work.) And it was through Cunningham that Catherine got the singular 1950 Creative Writing Fellowship (later the Stegner Fellowship) at Stanford, where of course Winters taught. Allen Tate was also at the University of Chicago, as a visiting professor, in 1949, while Catherine was there, and, while he was a less important influence than Cunningham, he lent his then-enormous authority to her early espousal of formal prosody and diction.

Experimentation and liberation, even transgression, were the essence of the early-20th-century Modernism I had been taught at my state school. Eliot and company were all about overturning the formal conventions shared, whatever their other differences, by Victorian and then Edwardian and Georgian poetry. "To break the iamb, that was the first heave," in Ezra Pound's words.

So the renewed poetic formalism of the 40s and 50s came as news to me. In the Workshop we were exposed to, and later encouraged to write, villanelles, among other archaic fixed forms. (And you may notice that, to this day, poets who have come through the Iowa Writers' Workshop tend to have villanelles, and often sestinas, to their names. "After a Time" is Catherine's villanelle.) By the time of Catherine's arrival in Iowa she had already achieved considerable expertise, one might well say mastery, in such forms and techniques.

It was in this context, I think—technical mastery—that Catherine said that she would settle for being remembered as a "minor poet"—a high designation for her, "poet" of any magnitude encompassing mastery of a degree not even imagined by any number of writers willing to call themselves poets, and the major poets being few indeed. (John Berryman, who was also a protégé of Tate, made a similar remark, raising the possibility that it was Tate's observation in the first place.)

But at this point Catherine was ready to move in a new direction, expanding rather than contracting. William Carlos Williams in particular had been a revelation for her, his work a liberation. We shared a love of his poetry, and talked about it at length, though she of course knew it far better than I did. She especially loved the devastating "To Elsie," with its arresting opening, "The pure products of America / go crazy." Possibly Catherine identified with the whole poem, being one of those "pure products" herself, like the Williams housemaid to whom the poem is dedicated. But the closing lines were the ones that moved her most deeply: "No one / to witness / and adjust, no one to drive the car."

In Williams she found not only looser paradoxes, but also a different variety of technical rigor, I think, though I don't recall her ever putting it in those terms. He practiced a precision of observation; in place of the grave, formal diction that characterizes her earlier poetry, a contemporary, often colloquial language, a new and inclusive but no less exacting diction. Above all, his free verse was energized by his amazing line breaks. I remember her talking with enthusiasm about his triads, which she can be seen practicing in "Railroads."

Catherine did not talk often about her private life prior to Iowa City, but when she did the elements remained the same: nostalgia for life with a beloved companion seen in the idealizing light of memory and absence. For five years she had lived in D.C. with Beth Nelson, who in conversation needed just one name, as if there were only one Beth in the world.

Beth was allergic to dogs, so they got a hypoallergenic dog, a basenji. Catherine was pleased with the solution, and with the dog. To hear her tell it, the years with Beth were harmonious because the central conflict had been removed. Beth confronted her with an ultimatum: give up drinking or give up the relationship. "*That* was simple," Catherine said. So for five years she stayed sober. She did not say what happened at the end of that time, but she took full blame for the relationship's dissolution.

Her earlier life she talked about less, other than to say that her mother made a boyfriend of her. To that she attributed her own sexuality, though without resentment. In that respect, at least, she possessed a matter-of-fact self-acceptance.

Despite the acceptance of grief expressed in Catherine's poems, a resignation to the point almost of world-weariness, she remained essentially hopeful during the time I knew her—or, if that's too strong, say she retained a sense of possibility. And she was, after all, only in her early 40s. After she got jobs at Pomona and then Kirksville, she seemed well-launched on a teaching career that would support her writing. (See her poem "Teacher.") She met Marie and her life became promising once again.

Even before that she was a romantic in the personal realm. When I returned to Iowa City, it was to live with a man twenty years my senior, a man Catherine's age who was also her long-time friend. She was as fiercely loyal to her friends as to her most beloved teachers, and she was worried when I told her I was breaking up with Gerald, moving out. She was protective of him, and ready to blame me or try to dissuade me. But I told her that I had asked him if he loved me, and he had replied, "Well, I used to …." That was enough for Catherine. She believed in love, and if love—amorphous, indefinable, ever-changing—was gone, then parting was all that was left.

I left town soon after, then so did Catherine, and by 1970 a sizable handful of people who had been friends in Iowa City had found themselves in Boston. I seldom saw Catherine, but do remember her reading new work to a group of us. She had finally captured her mother in the poem "She," where her debt to Williams is maybe clearest. She was pleased at how much we liked it. The poem was included in several editions of Mary Anne Ferguson's long-lived teaching anthology, *Images of Women in Literature*. I taught "She" numerous times, appreciating it more each time. (I wish "Second Thoughts" had been included, or that I had even known about it.)

Unsentimental poems expressing a self-aware ambivalence toward one's mother were not exactly common, especially in the 70s. That poem, probably her most widely-known by virtue of its inclusion in a textbook, always got strong student reactions. And always some students were taken aback, even shocked, that anyone could have such a critical distance on what was supposed to be the most beloved parent. "[T]he good die / young so / she kept going," Catherine wrote long years before Billy Joel. And in some ways even more discomfiting is the sardonic ending: "she gave as / good / as she got / and / here I am."

After that year we stayed in touch in the usual desultory way. And occasionally I would hear about her from some mutual friend, not always good news. I must have let Catherine know when my son was born in 1973, and there was at least one Christmas card later that decade. From Warsaw I wrote her in Boston, reporting on the reception of various American poets by my Polish students, in the early 80s when I was teaching there as an exchange professor. I told her I thought of her much more often than my sketchy correspondence would suggest. It was true. I wrote that I was "realizing that I am the same age you were when you were rediscovering him [Williams] in Iowa City. I remember your excitement vividly, and you are, forever, I guess, implicated in the poems for me" (8 March 1984). She wrote to make sure

I knew Williams's poem "Heel and Toe to the End," on Yuri Gagarin, the first man in space.

Absorbed in my own life, I did not know when she died. I am sorry. I would have liked to celebrate her then. I celebrate her now.

NOTE

[1] Bottum, Joseph. "America's Best Forgotten Poet: *The Poems of J. V. Cunningham.*" *The Weekly Standard*, February 16, 1998.

LOOKING IN AND LOOKING OUT

Martha Collins

I first encountered Catherine Davis at the University of Iowa when Mark Strand asked her to lecture on diction in a course he was teaching called Form of Poetry. Although it was not "the workshop," I think I was the only person in the class who was not an MFA student—who was not, in fact, even a poet yet, but only an English graduate student whose love of poetry had convinced her that she shouldn't go to law school after all.

Davis was older than most of the other workshop students, and had something of a reputation because she had been anthologized in Hall, Pack and Simpson's *New Poets of England and America* (these were the days when publication was not expected of MFA applicants). She lived up to her reputation in the class, which, to my ears at least, was brilliant: going back to the Renaissance and up to something near the present, Davis distinguished plain and aureate styles—and in the process evoked, for me, the spirit of Yvor Winters, which had presided over the Stanford English Department from which I and my then-husband had just graduated. After I learned that Catherine had been there many years before, she, my husband, and I struck up a friendship based partly on that coincidence but more on Catherine's intelligence and knowledge of poetry. No strict Wintersian—few of his students were—she had nonetheless absorbed from him, as we had, the idea that poetry was somehow *important.*

In my subsequent years in Iowa City, as I drifted in and out of graduate school, Catherine became not exactly a mentor, but at least an example and sounding board. My first attempts at poetry were halting, uncertain, but her lessons were clear. I remember three. The first, when I dared to show her something I'd written: "Some people would consider that a poem" (I of course paraphrase, all these years later). The second, when I had written a little more: "You can write poetry if you want to. But you'll have to work at it. When you decide to do that, I'll be happy to read what you write." The third lesson came much later, after I had indeed decided to "work at it." At this distance, I can't remember how much of it came in words, how much by example. But it went something like this: Don't do as I have done. If you care about your poems, you should try to publish them.

Not that Davis didn't try, in fits and starts. But many of today's young poets would be appalled by how little effort she made, and how little she made of her "connections"—although it was almost always those connections that prompted her to send work to magazines and presses. Seriously complicating the situation was the fact that her shift from formalist to free verse poet, never total, was not as smooth as that made by others in her generation, despite what she wrote in 1994 in "The Air We Breathed."[1]

I witnessed some of that transition, beginning in Iowa City but continuing more significantly when, after teaching in California and Missouri, Davis came to Boston in 1968. I was on leave that year from UMass-Boston, where she would later teach, but I began to see both her and her work again when I returned. It's been a privilege, this past year, for me to go back to the poems, most of which I hadn't seen for decades—on the one hand with the excitement of rediscovery (oh I had forgotten that line!), on the other as if I were seeing them for the first time. I've had the additional pleasure of reading through Davis's notebooks, which I'd almost never seen, except across a table or room when she was writing in one (as she often was). It's with this complex vision that I read the poems now.

————◆————

If Catherine Davis subscribed to "plain style" diction, this did not mean that even her earliest poems were themselves very plain. For one thing, "plain" did not mean conversational, easy; it meant precise, concise, with every word counting. Nor did it mean simple: committed to exploring deeply, Davis traced patterns of complex thought through what was often quite complex syntax. And her poems *did* explore deeply, not stopping before she had arrived at a place that was often quite different from the place where she began.

Because we live in a poetic age when neither the plain style nor strict formalism is in fashion (not to mention abstraction, that workshop no-no), it may be easy for some to ignore Davis's earliest work. But rereading after all these years, I'm struck by how much is actually *happening* in these apparently static poems, and by how much more happens upon subsequent re-readings. While "Routine," "Patience," etc. may sound like definition poems, a careful reading involves one deeply in states of mind that are simultaneously states of feeling. It's partly the interplay of prosody, syntax, and diction that makes this happen; but it's also the refusal to settle for less than a full exploration of experience.

Consider "Obsession," which, addressing its subject as a "parasitic ghost" that eats the speaker's "substance," continues: "You share my narrow bed; you make / My thoughts your own, your own my blood." The enjambment is one of several in the poem that provide an appropriately complicating counterpoint to the iambic tetrameter, even as the syntactic inversion creates a near-chiasmus that encapsulates the nature of the relationship. The third stanza has another compelling line break, which forces us to contemplate the striking simile before going on to the important "and":

> That you are nothing, yet exist!
> You feed as shadow on the light
> And grow—on what shall I subsist?

Rather than answer its own question, the poem expands exactly halfway through, and the already terrifying "obsession" does what—it seems to me on reflection—

obsessions indeed do: "You multiply before my eyes ... / Sit in the fixed mind and devise / Your own malign loose shapes of terror." Here, the metrical variations and enjambment convey the disturbance that the growing obsession creates until the "loose shapes" become, in the next stanza, "Innumerable mouths."

Or consider the much quieter "Routine," which begins: "Oppressive hours and days and years / Of days and hours of this routine." Like this chiasmic repetition, the poem's shift from tetrameter to trimeter in each of its three quatrains' final lines slows the poem to the point that we experience, aurally, how (moving here from the second to the third quatrain) "The sense of weight delays // The sense of time."

The plain style demands care, and Davis chose her words carefully. And having chosen, she sometimes let them move her through a poem. In one of her epigrams, "Kindness" (Insight 4), seven variations on the title word appear in the ten lines of the poem, which ends by evoking two additional—well, kinds of kindness: "That would be kindness of a kind, / To be again of a like mind." Or, somewhat later, "The Summer Leaves": apparently a noun, and indeed the subject of the poem, "leaves" becomes a verb as the poem moves into its first line. In the last two lines, the poet has it both ways, with "the summer leaves / again" suggesting mostly (the verb) loss, but also (the noun) the possibility of "again."

The syntax throughout "The Summer Leaves" is complex—here, as in other poems, not as a concession to form, but as an enactment of what the poem is conveying.

"The Years" is similarly elaborate in its syntax, beginning with the suspension of what appears to be an intransitive verb at the end of the second line: "Then came the year of fires. The burnings always took—" But the dash introduces what turns out to be an interruption of the main clause, which adds an object three lines later: "took ... the form of lost desires, / Of purification rites." Thus what began as an evocation of actual fires becomes a trope for something else. In the similarly complex last stanza of the poem, the back-and-forth syntax forms a kind of parallel to the "looking in / and looking out" to which the poem refers.

"Looking In and Looking Out" ultimately replaced "Insights" as the title Davis gave to her ever-changing collection of epigrams, and, in 1998, also became the title of her only published chapbook. There is in fact some chronological movement in her work from "looking in" to "looking out." The first manuscript she arranged, following her MA thesis, was called *From the Narrow House to the Wide World*; the order of the poems, roughly chronological, reflects that movement. It's important to note, though, that while some of the early poems, including "Obsession," use a sustained metaphor, many others begin by "looking out" at the physical world, however briefly. This is the case with the early poem "The Leaves" (which makes me more deeply aware of the relation between physical light and shade than I am inclined to be), and even "Routine," with its "office dust in morning air."

But the physical world becomes increasingly *visible* in the poems Davis wrote after she hand-printed the last of three pamphlets of her poems in 1962. The final poem in that pamphlet, "Late," seems to me to mark a kind of transition. While they evoke Yeats and are "Calm emblems of unprecedented loss," the swans in the poem—"steering through dark channels," their "necks outthrust or arched like ancient prows"—are fully present, as much themselves as they are (simultaneously) something else.

In "Out of Work, Out of Touch, Out of Sorts," the formula tilts a little more in the direction of "looking out" as Davis carefully observes a Dupont Circle fountain before expanding the scene to an earlier time and making of it, through suspended syntax, a trope for her own thought—all without ever losing the sense of place that grounds the poem:

> All winter long this scene—
> The walks, spokes of a wheel,
> The civil white and green
> Of everyday concerns,
> The Circle like a reel
> On which the gigantic thread
> Of traffic sings and turns,
> The staid fountain's commotion—
> Turned in my mind and brought,
> For every move that led
> Forward, a quicker thought
> In steady countermotion.

The "countermotion" takes the poet to "the past" in the next stanza, picking up the winter scene as metaphor ("The long, eccentric snow / Of being somewhere else / Falls through perfect weather"); in the next, "the shadow of events," the "downward slope / Of a decade's near-disaster" expand the scope of the poem further, beyond the self. But much as a careful setting in a Henry James novel can locate us for pages of internal reflection, we continue to experience the poem while sitting with the poet in Dupont Circle.

The Washington poem was finished if not altogether written after Davis arrived in Iowa in 1961, where she continued to "look out." "An Ordinary Sunday Morning in Iowa City" simultaneously evokes the small town itself and a mood, using colloquial language ("One phones, but no one's there or nothing doing"; "The day has nothing up its sleeve but rain") that perhaps parallels the distance Davis's work had by then traveled toward the world of everyday experience and discourse.

The outward movement is also reflected in the title of another Iowa City poem, the marvelous "A Small River in Iowa and the Wide World." A counterpart to "Out of Work ...," "A Small River" begins similarly ("July, late afternoon, I sit alone / And look ..."), but then moves through immediate time until "the sun is gone." Evoking "three perfect oval mirrors" cast by a "homely bridge's arches," the poem itself becomes a "reflection" on perfection and imperfection, permanence and impermanence, and, in its final phrase, "earth's both excellence and plunder." Throughout, Davis weaves observation and contemplation: "the fire-swept wings of the blackbirds, the flood / Of feelings that their shadows on the grass / Give rise to, as the day flames down, turns slate." An elegantly formal poem in iambic pentameter, with each stanza repeating an *abcabc* rhyme scheme, the poem at the same time omits punctuation to produce, for example, "a knot / Of spirit bones flesh blood dark love loss gall," and is also more personal and even colloquial in its address to someone else than much of the earlier work: "Then what of me? of you?"

The sonnet sequence *"for tender stalkes,"* begun in 1964 and added to at least as late as 1970, also reflects this movement toward the personal, taking as its immediate impetus an "unpromising" love "so wasting and distraught, / It let me neither work nor rest." Davis had addressed love in general (and sometimes witty) terms before ("Love is not blind, but overmuch / Given to darkness goes by touch"). But the address to "you," as well as the movement through some vicissitudes of love (in the tradition of Shakespeare and others), indicate a willingness to reveal feeling in more immediate terms, even as they lead to some of Davis's most eloquent verse:

> Our bodies are the graves and churches
> Where being near unbeing dwells;
> Love meets here what it likes, dislikes,
> Bends down, of two minds, strokes and strikes,
> Finds in the good for which it searches
> The dark it gathers and dispels.

A somewhat later manifestation of the more personal lies in Davis's exploration of the past, which, like love, had appeared in abstract terms in a number of even the earliest poems, but was not given names and faces until the notebooks of 1970. "Message," originally an "Insight" addressed to "C.D.M.," is later addressed to "Dear Sister"; its concluding reference to "the past you fled" thus directs us to Davis's own past, which she explores in at least two finished poems, and which she also attempted to write about in a number of unfinished poems and additions to poems.[2] The beginning of all versions of the much revised "Railroads" ("Railroads / run through / my life") takes us immediately into the particulars of her life, early and late, and in its final version includes a surprising amount of detail, including the following passage about Buck Dillon's mother's house, where she, her mother, and her sister lived:

> Buck Dillon! I see you staggering home at dawn to brawl
>   to meet spirit-breaking taunts with body-bruising blows.
> You always took the yearly Pledge after a three-week binge.
> But once while my mother raged
> you carefully dropped each supper dish on the floor
>   breaking them one by one for every curse of hers
>   your repartee all action
> until at last she stopped—the table cleared.

"She" turns to that same past, focusing on Davis's mother in colloquial terms ("what a hell / on wheels she was / but / drive!") and using what seems to be a description of the mother's actual driving to explore her character. Somewhat like the use of "The Leaves" in an early poem of that title, the immediate thus becomes not simply metaphor or symbol, but an image so deeply infused with something else that it functions, throughout, on two levels at once: "a good / head on her shoulders / quick reflexes / but no / spare or / no brakes at all / a welter of / signals and signs."

The fusion of tenor and vehicle in this poem is reminiscent of some poems by William Carlos Williams, including "Queen-Anne's-Lace"; and the form—while uniquely Davis's own, with its " blind / curves / hairpin / turns"—has a trace of Williams' triadic foot, which is clearly the formal basis for the first several versions of "Railroads." In "The Air We Breathed," Davis acknowledges the influence of Williams' *Pictures from Breughel,* which is clearly behind these poems, as well as shorter ones like "Teacher" and "Begging for Change."

The echo of Williams is easy to see—and hear—in most of Davis's free verse. This is not surprising. Although I don't recall that her lecture on plain and aureate styles made mention of him (her notebooks suggest that she really discovered him only in 1963), Williams would clearly have been in the former camp, and may have appealed to Davis on those grounds. After she moved to Boston in 1968, she continued to write formal poems, but by 1970 was writing more and more free verse. The style of many of these poems—without the tension created by the counterpoint of meter, rhyme, and syntax, and also without the tension of enjambment that dominates "She"—is surprisingly direct.

"Second Thoughts," the poet's own response to "She," is one example of this; others are most of the sections of *"The pure products of America,"* an eight-part sequence written in 1974–75 that she called, in a letter to Michael Van Walleghen, "free verse epigrams." Quoting Williams' "To Elsie" in its title, the poem consists of eight short sections, six of them taken from the news.[3] Here is the first, "Inside Out," which gains resonance if you know that Davis's own father was imprisoned for much of her childhood:[4]

> At the Iowa State Penitentiary, a man
> who was born in prison and had spent
> most of his forty years inside
> appealed to the governor to commute
> his parole to life imprisonment.
> Denied, he left, once more, for the outside

in a brand new suit with fifty bucks,
saying: "Well, here goes nothing."

These "free verse epigrams," like a number of other poems in the final manuscript Davis assembled, reflect an increasingly far-sighted "looking out" that actually began in the 1960s. The three-part title poem of that collection, "Yes Is a Very Big Word," was begun in 1964 (the same year as the sonnet sequence *"for tender stalkes"*), and added a coda in 1968; though its form seems to owe as much to accentual dimeter as it does to Williams, it shows Davis leaning toward both free verse and "events," several of which appear in the second section, "To an Archaeologist Some Years Hence." Beginning with white women protesting the integration of schools ("crowds of frightened / women jeering at / children"), the second stanza is an extended periodic sentence (syntax again!) that finally posits its verb after 24 lines: everything in the list "told us what we hated / but had to see."

If Davis's free verse in both her more personal poems and what we might call her more overtly "political" ones is not always stunningly musical, that may have been deliberate. A long poem dealing with her early months in Boston as a movie-ticket seller is called "The Combat Zone or the Poetry of Fact." It includes the lines "rather than face myself / I faced the facts. I read and read / and read *The New York Times, The Boston Globe* / trying to follow the anti-war's progression / the nation's regressions / transgressions," and continues: "But I couldn't see in all I saw and heard / a single line of poetry." It is important to note the bravery with which Davis finally did make poetry from contemporary topics that include poverty, war, and race: these were not dominant at the time (and for some remain suspect even now).

Nor did Davis restrict her explorations of this subject matter to free verse. She wrote a collection of "Jump Rope Rhymes for Hard Times" that apparently never made it out of her notebooks; and "The Summer That Never Was," begun in or around 1970, reflects on the assassinations of Martin Luther King, Jr. and Robert Kennedy, while at the same time recounting Davis's own troubled stay at a mental hospital the same year. This long poem, written in rhyming lines of varying metrical length, also displays—especially in its middle section—the careful "looking out" that Davis had been doing for several years. "The Willows in Winter in the Boston Public Garden," written in 1975, is a stunning example of both these practices.

Starting in the mid-1970s, Davis didn't finish many poems, and after 1977 apparently didn't complete any at all for seventeen years. The notebooks from the late 1970s contain a number of unfinished pieces, some in several versions. These include the free-verse poem "Blood, Flesh, and Bones," which ends after twelve lines of its third section with "(unfinished),"[5] and eleven lines of a sestina called "Mobile," which proposed to follow a 5-4-8-7-6-10 syllabic pattern in each stanza. Davis herself began to make mobiles sometime after this, and it would have been interesting to see what she would have done with such a subject in a form that itself turns "a thing that remains the same / Into something that changes."

———◆———

In the early 1970s, I moved for a time to a suburb south of Boston; after that, I saw somewhat less of Catherine Davis, even though, after 1974, we were teaching at the same school. Until I saw the notebooks and later manuscripts this year, I didn't know much about what she was writing (although I had seen some poems from 1974-75), and I wasn't aware that she had quit writing new poems after 1977. I did hear about her from Donald Justice, up into the mid-1990s: every time I saw him he mentioned their frequent telephone conversations, her increasingly impoverished circumstances, the fact that she was compiling a selected poems. Implicit in these conversations was a wish that I—closer, in New England—could help, but by then I couldn't: I hadn't seen her since the early 1980s.

A note about me in a 1980 journal reads: "not much of a personal relation anymore," and that was true. But that same year, when a group of my poems appeared in a "Feature Poet" section of the *Agni Review*, I left a copy in Catherine's school mailbox, with thanks to her for her support over the years, and in turn she left me a note. Generously telling me which poems she "*very* much" liked, she went on to say that the first four stanzas of another poem were "very good, too," but that "for me the last two stanzas throw the poem off. Would a more oblique approach here be better?" After some final comments about the poem she liked "least," she closed by saying "so much was good, funny, clear, and fresh that I was (am) *happy* to see the poems."

That is who Catherine Davis was for me: someone who was alert to the smallest nuances and blunders of my poems (she was absolutely right in that note: I'm embarrassed, now, by the stanzas and lines she didn't like), but who was always happy to see them. I've somehow known that, all these years, but now I wonder whether I would indeed have decided to "work at it" if it hadn't been for her.

More specifically, it has occurred to me as I've reread the poems that my abiding interest in syntax was deeply influenced by Davis. So too, I realize, my love affair with dictionaries, both mental and actual. Inclined from childhood to hear echoes of words in other words, I remember the delight with which I first encountered all those kindnesses in Davis's early epigram, or later read, in "A Small River in Iowa," of " a moment's wonder / That fails as morning's dew, as mornings do."

In 1994, while compiling her selected poems, Davis finally completed a new poem (one I hadn't seen until this year). And at the end of her last notebook, dated 1998, "Finding a Way" appears. Probably a revision of an earlier poem, it reveals, I think, something about the strategies of much of her work, and also something of what she subtly taught me about the function and importance of poetry:

This, it may be, is one way
That the interstices
Of sound and thought and feeling
When all else is unease
Might be given continuous play.
We would possess
The inexpressibly near,
Stealing
From distance, by formal means,
The unclear,
Immediate, fugitive in-betweens.

Like so much memorable poetry, Catherine Davis's dwells in those "fugitive in-betweens," peering now one way, now the other, but always looking in and looking out, using syntax, form, layered imagery, and nuanced diction to connect—in the words of her early manuscript—"the narrow house" and "the wide world."

NOTES

[1] See pp. 197-198 of this volume.

[2] The notebooks contain numerous attempts to add to what was later called "A Small River in Iowa and the Wide World." Breaking after the fourth stanza in most of these attempts, a second numbered section begins: "I think of all of the scattered cities I / Have tried to live in"; three stanzas later, following "(unfinished)" and a large blank space, it continues: "The time was always many years ago; / The place, Sioux City." This version, including the gap, was included in at least one manuscript Davis assembled.

[3] "Begging for Change," on p. 87 of this volume, is the second section.

[4] Davis never included her father (whom she didn't see after he went to prison) in a finished poem, but she wrote several lines in 1977 for a poem that was undoubtedly intended to parallel "She":

HE

is the fixed wanderer
                    who always comes back
        but never shows up
                    in the common light of day

[5] See pp. 202-205 of this volume. Davis included this poem, with "(unfinished)" at the end, in at least two of the manuscripts she assembled.

THE AIR WE BREATHED

Catherine Breese Davis

Poets of my generation did not consider formal poetry an anomaly. Rather, it was the air we breathed. In our younger years many of us were reading Wallace Stevens, Marianne Moore, Ezra Pound, T. S. Eliot, e. e. cummings, and Hart Crane, most of whom had written both formal verse and free verse. The exception was William Carlos Williams, who, at least in his known published work, wrote only free verse. On the other hand, W. B. Yeats, E. A. Robinson, and Robert Frost wrote only formal poetry. We were also reading, of course, the poetry of an earlier generation: Thomas Hardy, Walt Whitman, and Emily Dickinson. The generation that most directly influenced many of us, and certainly me, were, except for John Crowe Ransom, all born in the twentieth century and were not only our mentors but also sometimes

Reprinted from *A Formal Feeling Comes: Poems in Form by Contemporary Women Poets*, ed. Annie Finch (Storyline Press, 1994; reissued Textos Books, 2007), 51-52.

literally our teachers and advisers. In those early years the poets who deeply influenced me were largely formalists; they included, besides Ransom, the southern poets Allen Tate and Robert Penn Warren and, later, Louise Bogan, J. V. Cunningham, and Yvor Winters. All of the poets of whatever generation provided me and my contemporaries with the whole spectrum, from formal to free verse, of possibilities in writing poetry. It is astonishing to me now how little prejudice there was then about writing one kind of poetry over another.

The shift to free verse came, I think, in the early 1960s after the publication in 1959 of Robert Lowell's *Life Studies*, a book surprising in many ways from Lowell, a passionate traditionalist, not least because of the prominence of free verse in it. Then in 1962 William Carlos Williams' book *Pictures from Brueghel* came out. Both books had, I believe, a tremendous influence on the poets of my age. By that time, having finally received my B.A. at the age of thirty-seven, I had come as a graduate student to the Iowa Workshop, and it was an important change for me in every way. I began to write, much to my own surprise, free verse while continuing to write formal poetry; others changed to free verse for good. As the decade went along it was formal poetry that began to seem an anomaly, and it has been pretty much that way ever since. But I could never see why I should not practice both, as so many poets had done in the early twentieth century. Neither one is superior to the other.

NOTEBOOK ENTRY FOR UMASS-BOSTON CLASS PRESENTATION

2/11/79 for Pam Annas Practical Criticism class:
how "The Passing of Eden" evolved

> Sept.-Oct. 1965 – first version for "These Presences,"
no title. Immediate impetus: article in Cal Poly student
newspaper, reporting that what was thought to be "theft" of
roses in the rose garden was probably a case of deer eating
them. That—its inclusion in "These Presences"—explains
why it was written in syllabics; rhyme probably unintended
at first, merely happened upon when a rhyme came and I had
either to strike it out or continue rhyming. Hitting upon one
rhyme throughout probably also accidental—it occurred, and
then it seemed a dare—could I do the one rhyme, the length
of the poem? First version, 26 lines—probably thought it
would be shorter. Seemed perfect idea for a poem to GF; he
[seeming?] so forlorn in love

> In limbo, it seems, from 1966-77, during which time I
had more or less discarded "These Presences" and the poem
to Glen with it—the conscious rejection came in 1970 when
I saw a copy—probably Martha's—of the poem for the first
time in years. Remember being unpleasantly surprised by
how poorly the poem as a whole was written.

> In 1977 I tried to resuscitate the poem on Jeptha.
Must have had to do with "The Pure Products of America"
and the accident that the poem begins "We were both
discovering America." Then I saw again the possibilities in

the Esptein poem. Must have been because I saw possibilities in a separate poem with the title "The Passing of Eden." I remember my task seemed then to make the passage about the thieves clear—it was really murky in the earlier version (it came too late in the poem as well as not making clear what the situation was)—and probably to tighten up the "vision" passage. It was then, possibly from the experiences of rhyme changes, while trying to make another change in the poem, both good and bad—that I stumbled on "whispers of hooves" which changed, at least to some degree, both the meaning and the tone of the poem.

> Jan. 1979. I had improved the poem considerably in 1977, but I had also made compromises—most notably shifting "the price of roses here" to "the passing of Eden here"—again because of the exigencies of rhyme and syllable count (determined to allow no divergence from 7-syllable lines). Under the pressure of trying to get my poems ready for Don Justice's consideration—and maybe as a device for stalling with all the changes I wanted to make—I decided "just once more" to get it right. I had the brainstorm then of inverting "the whispers of hooves" and "as light as sighs" to "as light as sighs, the hooves among the roses." The irony is that I rejected this change in short order, but got down to revising the passages that were troubling me more. Final revision? Puzzled that none of these changes is in any notebook.

—CBD

THE PASSING OF EDEN
Pomona, California

To Glen Epstein

There are foxes on this hill,
friend, and rattlesnakes. But deer
also wander dreamily
among the palms, persimmons,
and cypresses and, I hear,
~~sometimes~~ browse on the Kellogg *Mansion* *sometimes*
~~Mansion~~ lawn, and ~~even~~ come
down at night when no one's near
to the rose garden below—
those profuse trim beds in bloom
summer and winter, all year
long, with ~~how many~~ roses, *— a feast of*
which ~~But for some time past~~, thieves or
perhaps vandals—out of mere
meanness was the common view—
had been ripping ~~them~~ off. I *read*
~~read~~ today ~~that it's now~~ clear *It's becoming*
who the culprits are. But O
the deer—I saw one ~~at last~~, *close by*
but fugitive, ~~a vision and~~ without peer
for ~~remote beauty and as~~ *remoteness —*
~~fugitive—~~know nothing ~~of~~
of the passing of Eden ~~here~~ *here,*
or the price of roses. ~~Still,~~
~~when I walk through the gardens,~~
I wonder now, will I hear
the whispers of hooves, as light
as sighs, among the roses?
What can we do when the deer,
half ~~cloud~~ visions all day, steal down
at night from the hill and eat
the roses and disappear?
                    --Catherine Davis

Still, whenever I linger
absently in the garden
now, I wonder, will I hear

BLOOD, FLESH, AND BONES

[an unfinished poem, c 1973-1976]

1.
The last time I sold my blood
it troubled me.

Twice, when it should have stopped,
it started to gush all over again,
and I do mean all over.

At first, I was quite surprised:
My bright red blood ran down my arm,
soaked through my clothes,
poured out and on to the floor,
and splattered the bright white uniforms
surrounding me.

After awhile, coat on and half way down the hall,
I felt my arm go hot, and I tacked—
Back to the room.
There, a bother of blood and gauze.
Then a long wait.

I was a little embarrassed.
Enough is enough,
and who wants to make a mess of things?

My blood, O negative, is a universal
donor but
recipient only of its own kind.

Reduced now to selling it,
I've never been a donor.
I'm a little embarrassed.

Finally, they let me go.
I made my way through the heavy corridors,
as careful
as an old
woman trying
not to rock
the boat
I found myself in.

2.

My flesh is beginning to grow on me.

When I was 37, I was as trim
as a miniature ship.
I felt like Mozart.

And I dreamed of a clarity
so intense
it would dazzle
the clear-eyed dew.

You'd think I'd have liked
the shape I was in. But I couldn't get over what I took to be
the simple location
of flesh.

And the clearness would always go
slipping
away
or end in an ocean of tears,
and the sea around me seemed
not half as rough
as the sea within me—

the list of all I thought was wrong
I thought
was interminable.

Now I am growing
almost comical.
My thighs begin to thicken, like a plot.
I can't keep up with my paunch.
If it continues the course it is on,
I hope it becomes
a belly-laughing sail:
so much itself
it is something else.

3.
I sometimes feel I've lost the little hull of myself,
the bare bones.
For years, they were the essence of me,
I thought,
a way of life,
like an over-serious poem, a perpetual

memento mori.
So I mostly kept myself on a shelf.

But now my brain,
which I used to think was my engine room—
it could really make things go—
seems a little out of control.

(unfinished)

PUBLICATIONS BY CATHERINE DAVIS NOT INCLUDED IN THIS VOLUME

Poems in Journals

Denver Quarterly: "Yes Is a Very Big Word," Parts 1 and 3 and Coda (1968)
Paris Review: "The New Year's Burden" (1961)
Poetry: "The Raven's Plight," "Plato and the Serpent," "Arachne: An Ode" (1950); "Cold Comfort" (1965) [available at poetryfoundation.org]
The Southern Review: "Seven Types of Clarity" (1964); *"for tender stalkes"* [seven additional sonnets] (1971)

Poems in Anthologies

The Glass Room, ed. Molly Matson (Library of the University of Massachusetts, Boston, 1977): "The Anniversary"
New Poets of England & America, ed. Donald Hall, Robert Pack, and Louis Simpson (Meridian Books, 1957): "Nausea"

Poems in a Chapbook

Catherine Davis, *Looking In and Looking Out* (1998): "World War II: Denmark, Angel Avengers"; seven epigrams not included in this collection, under the title "Looking In and Looking Out"

Reviews

Poetry: "The Texture of the Shroud" (February 1950); "Four Poets" (July 1956)

A NOTE ON MANUSCRIPTS

Aside from her University of Iowa thesis, the first full-length collection Davis put together was *From the Narrow House to the Wide World*, it included very little free verse. In 1970, she sent it to Frances McCullough, a Stanford graduate who was an editor at Harper and Row, but the publisher lost it and didn't ask her to resubmit; she also sent it to Knopf. A 1994 letter to Harry and Nancy Duncan indicates that she also tried "a few" contests—whether then or later isn't clear.

In subsequent years, Davis projected or actually completed several collections, including *Walking Around with Roger* (undated; 1970 title poem unfinished) and *Poems* (undated; complete collection in the papers). A 1976 journal note suggests that Harry Duncan considered hand-printing a collection of the work, not for his own Cummington Press but for Godine; and I believe there was later talk of Kim Merker printing a collection for his Windhover Press. Duncan and Merker were Iowa City printers known nationally for their fine-press editions.

In the late 1970s, Donald Justice asked Davis for a manuscript for the National Poetry Series, which, in its first year, was not yet a contest: five poets were asked to choose manuscripts by writers they knew. By this time, Davis had written a lot of free verse, and after much delay apparently sent two manuscripts: one of formal verse, one of free. (The latter may have been a thoroughly free verse manuscript dated 1977, *Railroads, Relations, and Others*.) She may have attempted to send a "selected poems" for the same purpose in 1979, when she received a note from Justice and wrote in her journal that "Time is running out." Justice himself told me that he did not receive a single complete manuscript from Davis and thus had to choose another poet for the series.

As far as I know, Davis did not send out a complete manuscript again until 1995, when she finished a manuscript of selected poems called *Yes Is a Very Big Word*; beginning and ending with formal poems, it included a great deal of free verse in the middle. Davis was in frequent touch with Don Justice throughout this period, and sent the manuscript to perhaps three university presses, at least one of which he had suggested. In the 1994 letter to the Duncans, she said: "I have had to wrestle with myself to do the book at all …. I'm not sure I would have tried so hard had it not been for Don Justice's timely encouragement." She did a great deal of revision for this collection, but was not satisfied with it and was not surprised when the presses rejected it. She wrote to Michael Van Walleghen that "it should have been published years ago. As it is, the ms. seems to be going in all directions."

Davis indicates in the same letter that beginning in the late 1970s she "couldn't finish any poem to [her] satisfaction and gradually quit writing," but that the process of assembling the manuscript had led her to start writing again, completing (as she said in the letter to the Duncans) a new poem for the first time in seventeen years.

After she sent the manuscript to the first of the university presses in 1995, she also sent a copy to Justice, "for safe-guarding." A year after that she wrote in her journal: "This may be an oddity (and I guess it is), but sometimes when I get exasperated with all this, I think the poems will all end in a black hole. I certainly don't want to have a posthumous book, but it may come to that."

—MC

CONTRIBUTORS' NOTES
& ACKNOWLEDGEMENTS

CONTRIBUTORS' NOTES

KATHE DAVIS retired from teaching women's writing and contemporary poetry at Kent State University, and now lives in a cabin in the Driftless region of Wisconsin. Her poems have appeared in *Blotterature, the Wisconsin Poets' Calendar, Parabola* (online), *The 2009 Lunar Calendar, Phoebe, Pudding Magazine*, and other periodicals; and in the collections *American Zen, Fresh Water*, and *A Gathering of Poets*, among others. She won the 2003 *Ohio Writers* first place poetry prize.

SUZANNE J. DOYLE has published the following slim volumes of verse: *Sweeter for the Dark* (1982), *Domestic Passions* (1984), *Dangerous Beauties* (1990), and *Calypso* (2003). For more than 25 years she has made her living writing for high-tech clients in the San Francisco Bay Area.

WILLIAM EDINGER retired from the English Department of the University of Maryland, Baltimore County with emeritus status in 2008 after teaching there for nearly thirty years. His articles have appeared in *ELH, Modern Philology, Literary Imagination* and other journals, and he has published two monographs on the literary criticism of Samuel Johnson, *Samuel Johnson and Poetic Style* and *Johnson and Detailed Representation*. He has received grant support from the American Council of Learned Societies, the American Philosophical Society, the National Endowment for the Humanities, and the Andrew Mellon Foundation. He is presently completing a book on Wordsworth, Coleridge and the philology of critical perception.

KENNETH FIELDS received his PhD from Stanford, where he studied with Yvor Winters. Since then he has taught in the Stanford English Department and the Creative Writing Program. He has taught the advanced poetry workshops for the Stegner Fellows in poetry, as well as a number of courses in poetry, film, American Indian literature, and the American Songbook. His books of poetry are *The Other Walker, Sunbelly, Smoke, The Odysseus Manuscripts, Classic Rough News, August Delights,* and a chapbook, *Anemographia: A Treatise on the Wind,* that is impossible to get. He is bringing together a collection of essays, *On the Loose,* and a book of poems, *The Hunter Deep in Summer.*

CAROL MOLDAW'S most recent book is *So Late, So Soon: New and Selected Poems* (Etruscan Press, 2010). Moldaw is the author of four other books of poetry, including *The Lightning Field* (2003), which won the 2002 FIELD Poetry Prize, and a novel, *The Widening* (Etruscan Press, 2008).

HELEN PINKERTON TRIMPI is a poet, literary essayist, reviewer, Melville scholar, and historian of the Civil War. She has published five books of poetry, including her selected poems, *Taken in Faith* (2002), and, most recently, poems and reviews in *Sewanee Review, Modern Age,* and *First Things.* In 1987, she published *Melville's Confidence Men and American Politics in the 1850s,* and, in 2009, *Crimson Confederates: Harvard Men Who Fought for the South,* a biographical cyclopedia. An interview with James Matthew Wilson about her poetry appeared in *Think Journal* in 2011.

MICHAEL VAN WALLEGHEN is a graduate of the Iowa Writers' Workshop where he was a classmate of Catherine Davis. He is currently Professor Emeritus of Creative Writing at The University of Illinois at Urbana-Champaign. He has published six books of poetry and another book will be ready soon.

EDITORS' NOTES

MARTHA COLLINS has published seven books of poetry, most recently *Day Unto Day*, *White Papers*, and *Blue Front*, as well as four collections of co-translated Vietnamese poetry. Her eighth book of poems, *Admit One: An American Scrapbook*, will be published in the Pitt Poetry Series in spring 2016. She is editor-at-large for *FIELD* magazine and an editor for the Oberlin College Press.

KEVIN PRUFER'S newest books are *National Anthem* (Four Way Books, 2008), *In a Beautiful Country* (2011), and *Churches* (2014). His forthcoming edited volumes include *Into English: Multiple Translations* (Graywolf, 2017; w/ Martha Collins) and, in collaboration with Wayne Miller and Travis Kurowski, *Literary Publishing in the 21st Century* (Milkweed, 2016)

MARTIN ROCK is the author of the poetry chapbook *Dear Mark* (Brooklyn Arts Press, 2013) and co-author of *Fish, You Bird* (Pilot, 2010). His work has appeared in *AGNI*, *Best New Poets 2012*, *Black Warrior Review*, *Conduit*, *Salamander* and other journals. The recipient of fellowships from NYU, the University of Houston, InPrint, and the Port Townsend Writers' Conference, he is Managing Editor of *Gulf Coast* and poet in residence at Texas Children's Hospital, where he writes poetry and stories with young patients and their families.

ACKNOWLEDGMENTS

The editors wish to thank Suzanne Doyle and Helen Pinkerton Trimpi, for the collection of Catherine Davis's poems they assembled, and for their help with this one; Marie Pelletier, for her constant help and guidance, and for permission to consult the notebooks, journals, and drafts of Davis's poems; Kevin Gallagher, for material from Joseph DeRoche's papers; and Roger Mitchell, for permission to print or reprint Davis's poems and other material.

Gratitude is also extended to the editors of the following publications, in which some of the poems in this volume first appeared:

Journals

Copper Nickel: "Teacher," "Railroads" (2015)
Denver Quarterly: "To an Archaeologist Some Years Hence" (1968)
Iowa Review: "The Passing of Eden" (1986)
Mead: "The Unprofitable Servant" (2015)
Measure: "Indolence," "Patience" (1950)
Memorious: "A Small River in Iowa and the Wide World,"
    "The Summer That Never Was" (2014)
The Nation: "The Summer Leaves" (2014)
The New Yorker: "Kindness" [Insight 4] (1955)
    [reprinted in *An Introduction to Poetry*, ed. X.J. Kennedy, 1966,
    and *The New Yorker Book of Poems*, 1969]
North American Review: "Out of Work, Out of Touch, Out of
    Sorts" (1964) [reprinted in *A Formal Feeling Comes*, ed. Annie
    Finch, 1994]
Paris Review: "What Does It Mean?" (1961)
    [reprinted in *The Heath Introduction to Poetry*, ed. Joseph
    DeRoche, 2000]
Plume: "The Willows in Winter in the Boston Public Garden" (2015)
Poetry: "The Leaves" (1950)

Poetry Porch: "Before You Enter," "Discretion," "Routine," "I Need
More Light," "Go" (2015)
Sequoia: "Under This Lintel" (1961)
Solstice: "Finding a Way" (2015)
The Southern Review: "The First Step," "The Narrow House" (1964);
"The Eumenides" (1968); *"for tender stalkes"* (1971);
"An Ordinary Sunday Morning in Iowa City" (1996);
"A Few Quiet Days," "Something to Be Said" (2015)

Anthologies

A Formal Feeling Comes: Poems in Form by Contemporary Women,
ed. Annie Finch (Story Line Press, 1994; reissued Textos,
2007): "Belongings," "The Years"
Images of Women in Literature, ed. Mary Anne Ferguson (Houghton
Mifflin, 1977): "She"
Iowa Workshop Poets, ed. Marvin Bell (Midwest/Statements, 1963):
"Obsession"
New Poets of England & America, ed. Donald Hall, Robert Pack, and
Louis Simpson (Meridian Books, 1957): "Insights 3-9,"
"Nausea," "After a Time"
["After a Time" reprinted in *Three Dimensions in Poetry,* ed.
Vincent Stewart, 1969, and *The Heath Introduction to Poetry,* ed.
Joseph DeRoche, 2000]
Quest for Reality, ed. Yvor Winters and Kenneth Fields (Swallow,
1969): Insights 10-14

Chapbook

Looking In and Looking Out (Robert L. Barth, 1998): "Insights 1-9,"
"Late," "Message," "To a Bottle," "Finding Ourselves and Others"